Twenty Minutes
a Day to a
More Powerful
Intelligence

Twenty Minutes
a Day to a
More Powerful
Intelligence

Arbie Dale, Ph.D.
with
Leida Snow

ꔮP

A Playboy Press Book

FOURTH PRINTING

Library of Congress Cataloging in Publication Data

Dale, Arbie.
    Twenty minutes a day to a more powerful intelligence.

    Bibliography: p.
        1. Intellect. 2. Mind and body. 3. Intellect
—Problems, exercises, etc. I. Snow, Leida, joint
author. II. Title.
BF431.D268   153   76–15276
ISBN 0–87223–460–6

To Robert John Murray R.T.S.O.T.B.
     and to Sam and Hedi

Contents

Acknowledgments

We are acutely aware, as we begin to write this, of how indebted we are to the many people who have come before in researching the hows and whys involved in enabling man to fulfill his potential. We would like to take this opportunity to express our gratitude.

Most of the time, we have been able to be precise about information and idea sources, but often we have chosen techniques and methods that have been reported by so many sources that all we can do here is to acknowledge that they are not original with us. It has not been our intention to come up with "new" exercises, but to demonstrate how to make optimum use out of what is there; in other words, to come at old information from a fresh point of view.

We would especially like to express my deep gratitude to the following people: Jeffrey Feinman, Alexander Lowen, James Weinland, Robert Ornstein, Robert Murray, and Earl Ostroff. We would also like to make it clear that although we have discussed exercises from many different sources and have explained thoroughly the difference between reading about them and doing them, it should also be acknowledged that experiencing some of them in the context of, for example, the *est* training would be a different kind of experience.

The authors note that they have chosen to use the personal "I" and "me" in writing this book. This is because they feel that they want the book to be seen as a personal message from a single source—intended for each reader individually.

Twenty Minutes a Day to a More Powerful Intelligence

———————◄•■———————

Chapter 1

Why This Book?

Every aspect of our lives today is saturated by concepts that are blithely discussed, yet only half understood. Advertising campaigns are said to be "creative," and to be geared to the "intelligent" consumer. Articles are written about "success-oriented" individuals. I believe that the carelessness with which these terms are used is destructive, because they seem to imply some fixed notion of what makes an individual intelligent or creative.

All manner of questions arise that I believe need to be answered. What is intelligence? What do we mean by education, by knowing? What makes one person creative and another less so? Is what we are basically fixed or what?

As though to underscore how little we actually know about intelligence, the *Dictionary of Psychological and Psychoanalytical Terms* devotes two and one-half tightly printed pages to defining it.[1] Here are the few definitions that I find instructive:

    1. Having the ability to deal effectively with tasks involving abstractions.

    2. Having the ability to learn.

    3. Having the ability to deal with new situations.

You will notice that I have not included ideas of measured intelligence as reflected in psychological tests measuring intelligence. Psychologists have long recognized the limits of these tests in determining functional intelligence; that is, how one actually confronts problems in real-life situations.

It is an obvious fact—yet one that is constantly forgotten—that all of the great and wonderful advances that man has made have been made in the face of the barriers of what was "known" to be true at the time. Some obvious examples are the explorations that led to the discovery of the New World (Didn't everyone "know" that the world was flat?); the discovery that the earth revolved around the sun; the inventions of the light bulb, the telephone, the airplane (Didn't everyone "know" that man couldn't fly?); and the breaking of the four-minute mile which everyone "knew" was an unbreakable barrier.

It is important that we make basic assumptions about our world and the way it works; otherwise there would be no stability to our lives. However, these assumptions then become barriers because it becomes difficult for us to perceive our world without them. In this way they may prevent us from reaching new understandings and higher possibilities.

This is equally true on the personal level, where it is important that we make assumptions about our individual capabilities. Here, too, these valuable assumptions turn into barriers that prevent our perception of our capabilities without them. In this way they may prevent us from achieving new understandings and higher possibilities for ourselves.

This book is predicated on the concept that you are the sum of what you make of your experiences. This is not the same as saying that you are the sum of your experiences. For example, if—when you were in grade school—your teacher told you that you were stupid because you flunked the mathematics examination, then what happened to you was that (1) you flunked the mathematics test, and (2) your teacher told you that you were stupid. That is what happened. The conclusions that you may have come to based on this experience, however, are myriad, because people internalize what happens to them in countless ways. On an unconscious level, you may have come to believe that your teacher was right, and this conviction would have followed you through life and influenced your reactions to the experiences that followed.

Everyone has a collection of negative conceptions about his personality and intelligence—impressions that limit achievement in very real ways and that may not be valid now if, in fact, they ever were.

Why do some people fulfill their potential? What makes certain individuals become what Abraham Maslow calls "self-actualizers"?[2] And what, exactly, does self-fulfillment or self-actualization mean in moment-to-moment terms? In other words, what do individuals who are fulfilling their potential actually do in their everyday lives?

What we are looking at here is the notion of self-fulfillment as an ongoing process. It is not some *thing* that you achieve or some *place* that you arrive at. Self-actualization means perceiving life as a series of choices and opting for the growth choice each time.

Perceiving life in this way means that one is coming from a position of responsibility about oneself and the world. This, in turn, implies the willingness to trust one's own perceptions so that one does not get lost in regrets and resentments about the past. Individuals who function in a self-actualizing manner experience fully, totally absorbed in the here-and-now.

Any behavior that makes it possible for the individual to tune in to what is true for him at the deepest levels is behavior that will enable him to come closer to self-fulfillment: You cannot actualize a self that has no reality for you. And that is what this book is about. It is also about the fact that realizing one's potential means hard work. It is enjoyable work because it concerns that which is closest to us, but it can also be demanding and arduous. People who achieve are hard workers.

One of the most interesting notions about self-actualizers is that they tend to have more "peak-experiences"[3] than non-actualizers. In this book, you will learn how to set up conditions so that these periods of insights and cognitions become more available to you.

As you begin to tune in to your own inner voices, you may find that you are learning to say "no" more. This may be because the ability to discipline oneself is related to the ability to say "no" to others, no matter how right they seem.

One way that we become aware of ourselves as individuals is by separating ourselves and perceiving ourselves as different from others. In a way, all "knowledge is a function of discrimination."[4] The more that one becomes cognizant of his own identity, the more able he becomes to oppose others in a constructive manner.

To truly know something else, one must first know oneself, and that, too, is what this book is about. It is also about doing and experiencing as opposed to passively letting information wash over you. Genuine learning is something that is experienced rather than simply intellectualized. That is, learning must be filtered through the total person and assimilated into the total being in order for it to be complete. Learning is more than simply collecting data and acquiring information. Information and experience have to be integrated into one's life.

How do we learn? This book is about approaching knowledge through logic *and* intuition. When we think of intelligence as purely rational, we are placing limits on ourselves and our capabilities. Again, this book is predicated on the notion that any analysis of intelligence must consider the processes of cognition and insight, and that knowledge that comes from intuitive sources has its place beside knowledge that is rational and explainable. The truly intelligent person uses both aspects of his personality, calling upon both the rational and the intuitive streams of knowledge.

It is the purpose of this book to show you ways to dramatically change your perception of yourself. Recent experiments have shown that you can change actual performance by transforming the manner in which a man habitually considers his performance.[5]

This book is very much about the possibility of change and about that urge to achieve that only a minority of people seem to exhibit. While some people are overwhelmed by considerations and situations, this minority feels challenged by opportunity and is willing to work in order to achieve its goals. What is the source of this need to achieve, and is there a technique that can be employed to give this will to achieve to people who do not exhibit it?

People who exhibit this will to achieve are found, in laboratory situations,[6] to set moderately difficult, but potentially achievable goals for themselves, and they also tend to place themselves, wherever possible, in positions in which they will be able to control or influence the outcome of the work involved. This book will show you methods through which you will be able to find out how to accomplish this.

Experiments have shown that people can, indeed, be taught to act like self-actualizers; that they can learn to set higher but realistic goals for themselves; that they can experience deeper levels of self-awareness.[7] Follow-up studies have demonstrated that the individuals who participated in these experiments had, in very realistic terms, achieved more than individuals who had not.[8]

This book will present proven, effective and creative techniques to expand your understanding of your own potential. It will show you ways to develop your powers of self-actualization. The methods described here can be easily comprehended and implemented, although most of them must be practiced for a time before they become habitual. The best part about them is that they work. All that is necessary is your time and your willingness to accept the new awareness that they offer.

Chapter 2

Twenty Minutes a Day

This book discusses a variety of ways in which you can develop your intellectual capabilities. Its purpose would be totally thwarted if you could not integrate its tenets into your life.

It is my intention to show you how to tap into an enormous reservoir of power that you may be only dimly aware of. To do this, you needn't spend vast quantities of time. What is required is a difference in the *quality* of time that you spend —not only in the doing of the exercises outlined, but in following suggestions that will modify how you approach your everyday activities.

For example, it may take you a while to approach new material in the ways suggested in the chapter on memory. But once you know how to learn in order to retain, you will actually be saving time. The same is true of almost all of the techniques and exercises explained in this book. Once you make them yours, you will not be using any special "practice time" on them. They will simply become the habitual way that you do things.

There are a few suggestions, however, that will need time set aside especially for them. These—such as those discussed in the chapters on motivated strengths and getting what you want from life—are not techniques that will have to be repeated daily. Although you will want to update your ideas about what you want from life periodically, for example, you need never spend more than twenty minutes a day unless you want to. And the difference in the way that you feel about yourself as you begin to get your intentions and desires clear will be well worth the effort that you put into this exercise.

There are a few techniques that will need some time from you on a fairly regular basis. However, having learned how to be in control of your time, you will have more time at your disposal, and so this should not be a hardship. In addition, although the suggestions outlined in the following pages will need your attention, they can be fun to follow if approached with an open mind and a real desire to learn.

You already possess this to some degree: You took the first positive step by picking up this book. Now decide that you will follow through. Not just by reading it, but by making it your purpose to use it—and that means doing the exercises and following the suggestions.

This book provides a unique opportunity because it combines many techniques in a step-by-step program that reveals their interrelationships and makes them easily assimilable. You will find the mystery being taken out of a lot of them. That has been my intention. It has also been one of my principal goals in writing this book to make many different techniques available in one volume. However, it should be noted that my purpose here has often been somewhat different from the originators of the techniques, and therefore my version of them is sometimes different.

The exercises, as I describe them, are geared always to the end of promoting expansion of consciousness, of self-awareness, of increased abilities. There is no exercise or technique that I have included that is to be viewed as an end in itself. As you proceed through the book, keep this in mind. It will enhance your understanding and your experience of what is intended.

What about the plan of the book? Well, first let me deal with the question of time. As I said before, one important distinction that I make is between quality versus quantity of time. I have chosen a twenty-minute time span because in my experience that represents a realistic goal: challenging, yet reasonable; moderately difficult, yet possible to obtain. You need never spend more than twenty minutes a day on any aspect of this book; however, what is required is that you devote *total concentration* during that time.

In practice what this means is that you set aside a period of twenty minutes entirely devoted to this book; that you take no phone calls during that time; that you do not have a radio or television set on; and that you set things up so that you will not be interrupted.

If this is totally impossible for you, then set up a ten-minute period or a five-minute private period to begin with. Come on now, anyone can find five minutes for something that can make such a dramatic difference in his life.

Naturally, if you want to spend more time, you may do so. However, be sure that all the time that you spend on this material is time that is totally focused, completely concentrated. Start right, and the rest will flow naturally from there.

If you genuinely do not see how you can set aside any time for total concentration, then you must look into your own motives. The tools are all here, but you cannot get the value out of them if you are not willing to use them.

All right then, you have decided to approach this material with full concentration. Now what? Well, my suggestion would be to start with a careful reading of the whole book in totally focused chunks of time. Use your twenty minutes simply to read and understand. For some of you this may be the first time that you will give something your complete attention. This, in itself, is a beginning of the training of your intellectual capabilities.

As you read, you may come across ideas that you can immediately incorporate into your life. Fine. Do that. Or you may come across an exercise that seems particularly intriguing or particularly enjoyable. By all means use your time to look into it. But my suggestion would be basically to steadily move through the book. Incidentally, read the exercises too. If you skim them now, your understanding will be muddled. What you are aiming for at this time is an intellectual grasp of the material.

At the end of the book, there is a chapter called "How to Use This Book." I have placed it at the end intentionally, because it is my feeling that once you have an understanding of what is intended plus the practice of reading in totally concentrated segments of time, you will be ready to experience the techniques described on a deeper level than you would if you approached the exercises directly.

Of course, this is only my suggestion. Naturally, you can read the book any way that you choose to. In fact, the material has been designed so that each chapter or unit can be approached individually, although the greatest benefits will be achieved if you follow the plan I have outlined. As far as the order of the material is concerned, I have put the chapters in an order that seemed to me to be the most helpful. However, if you have a special area that you want to tackle first, by all means go to that first. You may find that you will get more out of it when you return after having filled in what came before, but there is basically no reason why you shouldn't feel free to turn to your areas of strongest interest first (though always with total concentration).

Remember, this is your book. Make it really yours. Take a pencil in hand and underline points that you want to remember. Keep the book in a convenient place. This is material that is meant to be reread, to be used as a ready source of information.

Based on my experience in this field, this material—approached in this way—isn't only informative and helpful. Quite simply, it is enjoyable too. And I promise you that, if you follow the suggestions outlined here, your perception of yourself will change and the quality of your life will change. And you need never spend more than twenty minutes a day.

Chapter 3

About Energy

Early in this century, the philosopher William James published an essay titled "The Energies of Men"; its subject is one that has consistently interested philosophers and psychologists and is at the center of this book: namely, that *"as a rule men habitually use only a small part of the powers which they actually possess and which they might use under appropriate conditions."*[1]

Everyone has had experiences in which fatigue has been dispelled by unusual circumstances that called upon unexpected stored-up energies. Everyone has had the experience of "warming up" to a task. And everyone has had some experience with the phenomenon known as "second wind." Usually, at the first sign of fatigue, we decide that we have had "enough" and we stop what we are doing. But if some unusual circumstance prevents this, an astonishing thing happens. Yes, for a while we feel worse as we get more fatigued. But this only happens up to a point; beyond this point, the fatigue seems to vanish, and we feel refreshed and energized.

There is evidently a level of new energy available to us beyond that which we thought we had. Many layers of this experience may exist, perhaps a third and a fourth "wind."

Since this is true, the question that must be asked is this: How can we tap into these deeper levels, how can we live closer to our maximum capabilities? For the truth is, if we compare ourselves with what we *might* be, we are only half alive.

One of the most interesting points that James makes in his essay has to do with his comparison of nutritive equilibrium with what he calls "efficiency equilibrium." A man who is in nutritive equilibrium may eat differently every day, but his weight remains the same: his body equalizes his intake. The astonishing thing is that someone can be in nutritive equilibrium on greatly different amounts of food. Of course, you can systematically increase or decrease someone's intake of food and his weight will change accordingly. But the point is that there is a level beyond which he will neither gain nor lose any more weight on this altered diet. Once he reaches nutritive equilibrium again, his body is in balance, though at this new weight.

> Just so, one can be in what I might call "efficiency equilibrium" (neither gaining nor losing power once the equilibrium is reached) on astonishingly different quantities of work, no matter in what direction the work is measured.[2]

In other words, whether you are working on something physical, intellectual, moral or spiritual, your "efficiency equilibrium" can exist on many different levels.

Of course there are limits. You can only push the human organism so far. But the plain fact is that few people live at their maximum levels, and if you are energizing below your potential optimum, you are failing—by just that much—to make the most of your chance in life.

What are the ways to tap into these deeper levels of energy? That is what this book is all about. We will talk about the ideas and efforts that push us beyond what we habitually settle for. We will talk about what is meant by the "will," and we will talk about energy-releasing disciplines. We will consider fear and motivation, and we will talk about looking deep within ourselves in order to expand in all directions. In short, what we will be doing in the following pages is exploring many different ways to tap into those deeper levels of awareness.

In every one of us there are potential sources for power which we shut out because they do not conform to our belief systems. Throughout this book, I will be asking you to suspend disbelief—and also belief. There is no need to *believe* anything that I will be presenting here. What is necessary is only that you consider the possibility of the truth and the importance of the thesis that (1) we do not habitually live to the extent of our powers, and (2) that there are ways to liberate ourselves from our limitations.

Chapter 4

Perception

People say that "seeing is believing," but if you look into your experience, it is easy to realize how spurious such a statement is: Wasn't it just the other day that you were absolutely sure about something because you had "seen it with your own eyes," only to discover that, well, the facts weren't exactly what you'd thought they were?

Right now, take a moment and write down four or five sentences describing an apple in completely objective terms. As you write, do not use the word "fruit," and remember to describe what an apple is as objectively as you can.

What follows are some answers to this assignment, selected at random, by first-line supervisors who were enrolled in a training program that I conducted:

1. The object is round.
2. It is red.
3. It is delicious.
4. It can be eaten.
5. It is hard and firm.
6. It grows on trees.
7. I like it.
8. It is juicy.
9. It can be held in your hand.
10. It is pretty to look at.
11. It is sweet tasting.
12. It is fresh smelling.

Some of the above descriptions can be considered fairly

objective; most of them, however, are value judgments. Let me emphasize what I mean by going over some of the answers given above:

1. How many apples are perfectly round?

2. Is an apple totally red? Just how red is it? (Are *all* apples red? Define red.) What about the other side of the apple—the side that was blocked from your view. Is it also red? Or is it brown, yellow or green? Or is it spotted?

3. Is the apple delicious-tasting or is it a Delicious apple (compared to, say, a McIntosh apple, for example)? How can you tell if it is delicious-tasting just by looking at it?

4. How many things can be eaten? Other kinds of fruit? Animals? Fish?

Well, how did you do? Were your perceptions more objective than those listed? Or were they colored by your evaluations and feelings and opinions concerning apples?

All right. Now try this. Again, in objective terms, describe someone close to you—your husband or wife, your boss or best friend. Take the time to write down your description. Saying what you think out loud or thinking it over is not the same at all as writing it down. So take a few moments and do this.

Here are some descriptions, again made by first-line supervisors, who were asked to describe their bosses. (It should be noted that they submitted their papers to me anonymously.)

1. He is a bastard.

2. He is a nice guy.

3. He helps me when I ask him for assistance.

4. He is a "1,9" manager. (This description is based upon Blake's Management Grid.[1] It means that the manager or supervisor is concerned only with people and morale and not with production.)

5. He is a slave driver.

6. She expects me to do it right the first time.

7. She is both task- and maintenance-oriented. [Here the supervisor is using the vocabulary of the behavioral scientist, stating that the boss is interested in both people and production.]

8. He is fair.

9. He is rather an emotional person.

10. He is irregular in his performance.
11. He is a bright young man.
12. He is sensitive.
13. He has an interesting personality.
14. He is a hard worker and expects me to be the same.
15. He is ambitious.
16. He is determined to succeed.
17. He is inconsistent.
18. I would never buy him a beer, if that's what you mean.

Note, in particular, that each and every one of the above statements is a value judgment, and keep in mind that what was requested was a description in purely objective terms. Examples of objective descriptions would be the following:

1. He is a male.
2. He is over thirty years of age.
3. He always arrives at work before I do; he always leaves work after I do.
4. He has worked for the company for over ten years.
5. He has established rules for reporting grievances.

Notice the difference. Notice what happens to a perception when the evaluation is taken out of it.

Now for one more exercise before I define the term "perception" for the purposes of this chapter. This exercise is somewhat different from the preceding ones, and it concerns what happens when one person feels that he has been slighted by another. Take a moment and recall the last time a friend or acquaintance did not speak to you as you passed each other on the street. See if you can recall your reactions and your rationalizations. (Take the time to fully recall such an experience.) Did you assume that he was angry with you? Or did you believe that he simply had not seen you? How *did* you react? And most important, did you ask the other person if your perception was accurate? (That is, if you assumed that he was angry, did you *find out* if he was angry with you?) If you *did* ask him to explain his behavior, what did he answer? Could he have said something like, "I didn't even see you. I wasn't wearing my contact lenses at the time." (And you may not have even known that he needed corrective lenses to see!)

Let us turn now to the professional literature that deals with the concept of perception. This background material will

greatly add to your ability to understand the experiences of
the exercises of the following chapters.

Let us begin at the beginning: You see something; you then
make some interpretation. You see something; you report
about it (to yourself or to others on a conscious or unconscious level). In other words, perception is usually understood as encompassing both what your senses take in and
your interpretation or evaluation of whatever it is. Some other
definitions involve the following concepts:

1. The act of apprehending.
2. The understanding or view people have of things in the
world around them.[2]
3. The process of recognition.
4. The act of becoming aware of something.
5. A mental impression.

In other words, perception usually includes (1) responding
to cues which can be words, facial impressions, gestures and
specific overt acts; (2) making value judgments or forming
mental impressions; and (3) acting rationally or irrationally
on a conscious or unconscious level.

In order to test the accuracy of our judgments and impressions, we need to suspend this tendency to evaluate. This will
be considered in depth elsewhere, but for now let me simply
indicate what is required. Let us return to our example:

Cue: My friend did not speak to me as we passed each other
on the street.

Possible Value Judgments: He is angry with me.

                           He did not see me.

                           He has something on his mind.

                           He is sad, etc.

As you can see, there are a number of conclusions that you
might come to based on what actually happened (that your
friend passed you by without speaking). What is the solution?
It is a very simple one: Check it out with the person who
should know. Ask your friend what happened. Give him a
chance to explain before you "collect the injustice" and decide that you were snubbed.

In other words, the formula might be:

1. Perceive—see, hear, notice what happens.
2. Experience what happens minus your evaluation of it.

3. Check out the accuracy of your interpretation.

4. Then (and only then) act and react. Be happy or sad or angry or decisive based on what really happened . . . not what you decided happened. When you check out your perceptions, you are creating space for both yourself and the other person. This is what genuine communication is all about.

Zalkind and Costello, in their article on perception,[3] give five reasons why we misperceive:

1. We are influenced by cues below our threshold of awareness.

2. We respond to irrelevant cues.

3. We are influenced by emotional factors.

4. We are influenced by the weight of evidence coming from authoritarian sources.

5. We are unable to identify all of the factors influencing our perception.

An example of a cue that is aimed below your threshold of awareness would be the specific products that are used in motion pictures. We see an actor using a product while we are actually following the action. The product has nothing to do with the action, and it will probably be perceived only on a subconscious level; yet we may find that we then go out and purchase the product.

Another example of subliminal cues is reflected in our ability to recognize an object simply because of the context within which it is perceived. (Often, we recognize the doorman or the elevator operator because of the uniform that he is wearing.) It has also been demonstrated that a hungry person sometimes perceives food in a different way from a person who is not hungry.

An example of responding to irrelevant cues would be judging a person's job competence by the clothes he is wearing or the way that he speaks. Or you may relate a given facial expression to a given personality trait concluding that if a person is smiling, then he must be telling the truth; or that he is "shifty" because his eyes are close together.

The next time that you meet a person for the first time, see if you can separate out exactly why you like or dislike him in terms of your first impressions of him. In doing this, ask yourself exactly what cues you are responding to. If you are like most people, you will find that you are responding to irrelevant physical cues. One way that you can check this for yourself is to recall your first impression of someone you now know well. Is that what you thought he'd be like? How is he different from what you'd supposed?

When you are influenced by emotional factors, what happens is that you substitute an emotional response for a rational one: That which is liked or preferred is perceived as correct. And as far as investing authority with weight, usually it is a commonplace occurrence that we place more credence in a news item that appears in the *New York Times* rather than in a tabloid.

What usually keeps us from identifying all of the factors that influence our perception is that we are placing heavy emphasis on one or two of them. For example, when was the last time you spent an entire evening with someone only to discover that you could not recall anything except those two "unfortunate remarks" that he made?

Here is an exercise that you can do to deepen your understanding of the concepts of perception and evaluation:

Take some paper and briefly describe yourself as objectively as you can. The key here is the word objective. See if you can look at yourself as though you were perceiving yourself from the point of view of someone else. Of course this is difficult to do. But see if you can do it. Now, if you were an animal, which one would you be? What if you were a musical instrument? A food?[4] An interesting experiment would be to ask a friend to do this exercise about you and to compare the results. Another interesting experiment would be to put these answers away and return to them when you have been working for a while on the experiential exercises described in this book.

It is my intention to show you ways in which to deepen your awareness of yourself. Perceptual accuracy of others begins with perceptual accuracy of the self, and that is what this book is all about. There are many methods and techniques available that aim to develop your skills in these areas: sensitivity training sessions in industry; encounter and other forms of therapy; "mind-expansion" courses such as those offered by Silva Mind Control and *est,* and so on. All of these have something to offer because the concepts of perception (of self and others) and communication (with the self and with others) are so incredibly subtle and complex.

This book combines methods and techniques from many different sources, and its aim is to provide a synthesis of experience within which to expand.

One of the most important steps that you can take right now is to open yourself to the notion of the necessity for ambiguity. It is the intolerance for ambiguity, more than almost anything else, that prevents us from perceiving accurately. It is our insistence on some absolute "right" way to do something that prevents us from discovering *our* way to do it.

One of the implications of the concept of ambiguity is the willingness to see another's point of view with empathy and sensitivity. When you can genuinely see another's point of view, you have a much better chance of accurately perceiving the situation.

As you read through the following pages and experience the exercises that are described, see if you can delay evaluating what happens. The formula here might be:

1. Read and understand.

2. Experience minus your evaluations and judgments.

3. Check out the accuracy of your interpretation (in this case by evaluating your experience in terms of what it means to you).

4. Then (and only then) come to your conclusions.

Chapter 5

Meditation

The practice of meditation goes back centuries, and encompasses both the Eastern and the Judeo-Christian ethic. Many traditions and religions speak of a "mystic" experience or "mystic" consciousness. It is described in the Bible, in the Koran and in the writings of philosophers and poets. In this discussion we will, for the most part, steer clear of the mystical and mysterious and look at the effects that the meditation techniques have upon the physical body, the mental set and the emotional well-being of the practitioner.[1]

Right now—this minute—find a quiet place where you won't be disturbed. Give yourself five full minutes to sit absolutely still, in a comfortable—but not collapsed—posture. Have your breathing be regular and watch your breaths as they come in and go out.

Five full minutes later, answer this question truthfully: Do you feel the same? Or do you feel, in fact, calmer . . . somehow more in control? What about your thoughts? Do they seem somehow more ordered? Less diffused? It is especially interesting to try this exercise when your thoughts seem to be racing around—when you are upset about something, for example, or when you feel restless. Try bringing your body and breathing under your control the next time you feel you're running around in circles—and see what happens.

As with most of the exercises suggested in this book, the one just described has an effect that is experiential. That is, I can tell you about it, but until you experience it, you won't really get what I'm talking about although you may understand it on an intellectual level. So take the time now to experience the feeling that this deceptively simple exercise produces; it provides the foundation for a gut-level comprehension of what otherwise might seem abstruse and esoteric.

What do we mean by meditation? With all the current discussions, and words like "transcendental" and "kundalini" casually thrown around, it is still questionable whether a satisfactory definition of meditation can be given easily. Certainly meditation encompasses much more than what we intend when we say "I'll meditate on that," meaning something like "I'll think that over." What we are talking about here is a concept that refers to a set of techniques that aim at an intuitive rather than an intellectual knowledge, exercises that are designed to "produce an alteration of consciousness . . . [moving away] from an external focus of attention to an internal one."[2]

We are referring to what Abraham Maslow means when he discusses "plateau" and "peak" experiences that most people have had at some time in their lives. These altered states of consciousness were in the past considered to be available only as a part of religious experiences during which the individual having such an experience perceived the whole universe "as an integrated and unified whole." This is a concept that may sound simple, but it can have consequences of great magnitude for the individual involved.

> To have a clear perception (rather than a purely abstract and verbal philosophical acceptance) that the universe is all of a piece and that one has his place in it—one is a part of it, one belongs in it—can be so profound and shaking an experience that it can change the person's character and his *Weltanschauung* [character structure or way of life] forever after.[3]

Because of the non-verbal aspects of peak-experiences, it is not easy to describe what the individual actually experiences. However, certain themes are repeated when people describe what they have experienced at such times. They speak of the special cognitions and insights that they had, as well as a feeling of heightened concentration that is very different from any other kind of concentration that they are used to.

Words and phrases Maslow uses to describe what individuals report they feel during these cognitive experiences include the following: "loss of fear and anxiety," "ego-transcendence," "approach to non-striving," "integrative," "holistic," "a sense of being the creator of one's own experience," and "acceptance—even of evil." (This is similar to Werner Erhard's definition of experiencing the universe as perfect since perfection is "a state in which things are the way they are and are not the way they are not.")

Some people are definitely more receptive to peak-experiences than other people are. But, in any event, you cannot schedule or program peak-experiences. They are not the same at all as what happens through the use of drugs, even though sometimes similar results can be induced through certain drugs. On the other hand, what Maslow calls "plateau experiences" can be reached through work (i.e., meditation exercises), which can set up a receptive environment in the individual so that he can be more open to peaking.

In a very real way, we are limited in what we see by what we expect to see. In the same way, we are limited in our ability to experience fully by our conceptions and expectations of what will happen. Traditionally, the meditation techniques have been used to "dismantle the automaticity and selectivity of ordinary awareness."[4]

Research indicates that one of the aftereffects of the use of the concentrative disciplines is an ability to perceive freshly, to see things that we have seen many times before as though we were viewing them for the very first time.[5]

In other words, the doing of these exercises will have a consciousness-expanding effect. Experiments have proven that positive, long-lasting results can be achieved with consistent use of simple procedures.[6]

You can verify what is meant by this "deautomatization" that Deikman speaks of, by simply noticing what happens in everyday life. When you first walk into a restaurant, you may be aware of music playing and the noise of people talking; after a while, you no longer hear these sounds. Occasionally, you may be jolted back into an awareness of them, but basically your mind habituates to them. But with practice of the meditation techniques there is the possibility of maintaining a "consistent response to a stimulus which continues." Zen masters responding to a repetitive click over a period of time "responded to the last click just as strongly as they did to the first."[7]

All well and good, you say, but who wants to have to listen to all that noise? Isn't it better to be able to tune it out? The point of all this is not that you should have some chaotic din going on inside or that you should be unable to sort out visual, aural or other input. What is involved here is the availability of deeper experience. The meditative disciplines seem to offer us a way to perceive more, to see things with a fresh eye, to feel awake and alive inside.

A series of investigations, begun as early as 1924, demonstrate that if a situation is set up properly, processes in the autonomic nervous system that were thought to be beyond voluntary control can be seen to respond to self-regulation.[8] Recent reports and experiments document that yogis can control their blood flow and blood pressure and can lower their basal metabolic rate for hours on end.[9] Research has been done on self-control of muscle tension and of the activity of the heart; using equipment that provides a feedback mechanism so that the individual can become aware of what is going on inside him, he learns to exert a measure of control over his internal processes. Once someone has learned this kind of control, the feedback apparatus can be eliminated.[10]

These scientific experiments with biofeedback are rather primitive, but they have served to demonstrate to the scientific community the possibilities available through the procedures used in the concentrative-meditative exercises.

Exactly how do the meditation exercises work? That is, what do they do to affect consciousness? One area of research has been experimentally restricting the visual input a person experiences to a single, unchanging stimulus. This is accomplished by a system that allows the eye to move normally while a stable image is maintained on the retina. This, in effect mimics what happens in meditation, since all of the instructions for the concentrative meditation exercises indicate that whatever the object of meditation is, that and only that is the object that is to be allowed into the consciousness.

Individuals who participate in these experiments report the same experience of "blank-out," of a moment when the visual image simply disappears. Although, obviously, the comments of someone participating in a scientific experiment would have to be different from someone immersed in one of the esoteric traditions, nevertheless, it can be seen that the experiences themselves have essential things in common.[11]

As intriguing as the current research is, as fascinating as some of the results reported are, our main purpose in describing some of the meditation techniques will be to demonstrate how you can tap into that reservoir of intuitive knowledge that expands your awareness and opens you to new possibilities. In other words, how you can—through simple means—increase your intelligence.

What follows is in no way to be interpreted as a complete discussion of all the available meditation techniques. I have simply chosen those exercises that I have found to be most productive of results in a brief period of time. Let me emphasize, as I have before, that just the doing of the exercises will sharpen your mental skills, in this case by developing your powers of concentration and by changing your automatic way of looking at the world.

Savasana: This is a deep relaxation exercise taken from the Yogic posture meaning "dead man's pose." Lie on a somewhat hard surface, with legs comfortably separated and arms at your sides, palms up. Close your eyes. Breathe slowly and quietly for several moments.

Now bring your attention to your right leg and foot. Stretch the leg along the ground, point the toe and tighten all the muscles in your right leg and foot while slightly lifting the leg off the ground. Hold this tensed leg position for a moment and then let the leg fall to the ground. Move the foot loosely from side to side, let it come to a comfortable resting position —and forget about it. Go through the same procedure with your left leg and foot.

Now bring your attention to your right arm. Stretch out your arm and hand along the ground, lift it slightly off the ground, make a fist and hold the arm tense for a moment and then let the arm fall to the ground. Move it loosely from side to side, let it come to a comfortable resting position—and forget about it. Go through the same proceedure with your left arm and hand.

Proceed deliberately and steadily. You cannot rush this exercise.

Next, bring your attention to your buttocks and lower back. Tense the muscles of the buttocks until they are lifted slightly off the ground. Hold this position for a moment—and then release. Feel these muscles let go. Now bring your attention to the muscles in your stomach. Take air into your stomach until the stomach blows up like a balloon. Hold, and release. Next bring your attention to your shoulders. Keeping your head on the ground, bring your shoulders forward as though they could touch one another. This will lift them (though not your head) off the ground. Hold . . . hold . . . hold . . . and release. Let go of these muscles.

Now bring your attention to your face. Scrunch up your face as much as you can. Tighten all the muscles . . . hold . . . hold . . . and release. Now open your face as much as you can. Lift your eyebrows, open your mouth, your whole face open, open, open (except for your eyelids) . . . and release. Gently roll your head from side to side. Let it come to rest in the center. Relax.

Breathe slowly and steadily as you systematically go over your body. Wherever you notice tension just let go. Allow all of your muscles to relax. Allow the body to remain still throughout the remainder of the exercise. Continue to breathe deeply, quietly and slowly. Observe the breath as it goes in and out.

The next part of the exercise will entail using your imagination in regard to the concept of the "life force." In the Hindu tradition, the life force, or *prana,* is held to be that from which health and creativity flow. It is "the force which aids in physical as well as psychological growth."[12]

Continue to breathe regularly, deeply. During the inhalation, imagine the life force *(prana)* in the air being drawn into your body. If extraneous thoughts come, notice them . . . and return to concentrating on the breath and the life force. It may help to visualize the life force as a pure white light bathing your body and being drawn into it. Remember to allow the body to remain still and quiet during this exercise. Allow yourself to fully experience the stillness and the deep relaxation.

Guiding the Life Force: Sit or lie in a comfortable position. Completely relax, as in *Savasana.* Take your time: These subtle bodily changes cannot be rushed. Now, place your hands lightly on that spot just beneath and between your ribs. This is the solar plexus, or "sun center." Breathe evenly and slowly keeping your fingers lightly on the solar plexus.

Now see if you can imagine that as you inhale you are drawing into your body the *prana* that is in the air. Visualize this as intensely as you can. Feel the pure energy of the white light flooding through your body. Inhale deeply. Now imagine that all of this energy has reached your fingertips. Focus completely—feel the energy in your fingertips. Feel the heat of the white light. Concentrate intensely on it. When you have completed the inhalation, place your fingertips on your forehead. As you transfer your fingers to your forehead, hold the breath. Concentrate on transfering the *prana* to your forehead. Now, very, very slowly exhale—and visualize the energy flowing, cascading from your fingertips, filling your head. Imagine that now your entire head is filled, flooded with this life force. When you have completed the exhalation, slowly bring your fingers back to rest lightly on the solar plexus. You are now ready to repeat the entire process.

It is very important that throughout the exercise you retain the image of the pure white light of energy in your mind's eye. Imagine it. Visualize it. Create it. Keep it with you.

You can guide the life force to any area of your body that you want to. I have simply used the head as an example. For instance, if you have a muscle pain somewhere in your body, you would go through the same process outlined except that instead of transfering the life-force energy to your head, you would transfer it to some other part of your body. To feel the life force flooding through your mind and head, however, is especially valuable. The solar plexus, or sun center, is good to use as the starting point because it is thought to be a major center of the body and a major center for the storage of the life force.

Remember to take yourself through the various stages of this exercise slowly and with concentration. Go through the entire sequence of movements several times. It is only by experiencing several repetitions of the entire sequence of movements that you can begin to experience the optimum results.

This force that you are beginning to learn to guide is an incredibly subtle one, and therefore it may take some time before you can fully experience it. But even though it is subtle, it is also real. The air around us contains more than the components that we usually consider. There exists also an energy that can be available to us. This "pure, absolute energy" (another translation of the word *prana*) represents a force and intelligence that is present even in inanimate objects. The life force manifests itself in everything . . . it is at the core of the atoms that make up everything. According to this understanding, what varies is only the degree of vibration, the degree to which something contains this energy.

That is why we must encourage the guiding of this force, so that we can develop it within ourselves and expand through our experience of it.

For some of you this will be an easily accessible concept. For others it may seem like so much mumbo jumbo. I would like to remind these that there are sounds that the human ear cannot hear. So, too, with this powerful force. The human eye cannot see it, and yet it exists. My suggestion is simply to practice this and the other meditation exercises. As you do, you will come more and more to feel the reality of this astonishing force.

The Witness: This is an exercise in living absolutely in the here and now. It is an exercise in which you observe yourself as though you were another person. This is a matter of noticing exactly what you are doing at the precise moment that you are doing it—of investing ordinary activity with attention.

What this requires is that you be totally conscious of each action that you undertake. Usually people go through the motions of what they are about while their minds are actually concerned with something in the past or in the future. In this exercise, you observe, witness every action intently. You notice yourself stretching, standing, sitting. You watch as you move or talk or eat. This may seem very simple. It is actually one of the most difficult tasks you can undertake, because you are to simply *witness* what goes on with you without adding anything to it. The term "witness" is used to differentiate between observation and anything that is judgmental or active. You do not purposefully change your action or place a value on what you are about. You simply watch. You become mindful of exactly what you are doing in the present moment.

By the way, you needn't be involved in any high-minded activity in order to practice this exercise. On the contrary, the whole point is to develop your consciousness and awareness by paying close attention to whatever you happen to be doing. This "right-mindedness," as it is known in Zen, can be focused on any action whatever. It is a matter of being "mindful" of what you are about at the present moment. You focus close attention on each activity, whether it is brushing your teeth or opening a door, and this total absorption in the present moment serves as a way of expanding your consciousness and awareness.

Protecting the Life Force: Although the life force is very powerful, it is also easily dissipated. Any way that you can increase the efficiency of your motions and decrease the amount of effort you expend toward reaching specific goals will tend to conserve this valuable force. One way to learn how to stop wasting your energy is to look at yourself at unexpected moments during the day. If you stop what you are doing and examine what you have been doing, you may be surprised by how much energy you waste because of tension and unconscious or half-conscious nervous habits. You needn't be somber about this. Just remind yourself periodically to observe your body in action and notice where you are tense and how that tension manifests itself. Then quickly go over your body mentally and direct every area that is tense to relax. Be gentle and calm, but firmly direct your body to move towards relaxation. Eliminate useless, wasteful movements. It will be necessary to reeducate your body, but if you do this consistently, your body will respond.

Be aware of how you respond to people around you. If you notice that you always feel somewhat drained when around certain people, see if you can eliminate time spent with them. If this is impossible, then counter the time that you must spend with them by doing exercises to increase the life force (such as the ones discussed in this chapter). Whenever possible, be with people who leave you with an elevated, positive feeling.

Remember, it takes energy to hold your muscles tense, to counteract negative vibrations, to tap your foot or chew gum, to fiddle with reading material and television programs that are not stimulating. These experiences can drain and exhaust you. Your time and energy is too precious to waste on such things.

Every person is unique and what is a chore for one will be an uplifting experience for another. Take the time to look into yourself and find out what is good for you. If something or someone leaves you drained either physically or emotionally, then that is an activity or a person to be avoided whenever possible.

Of course we are all good rationalizers, and we tell ourselves that we will "relax" and watch some television. Maybe you can relax in this way. But be honest now. If several hours of television viewing leave you feeling limp and exhausted, then you have been working against your best interests in watching.

Meditation: In essence, meditation has to do with the idea of focused attention. One is instructed to concentrate on some source of stimulation that is unchanging. In a sense, every exercise that we have looked at so far has been a form of meditation. Meditation can involve vision or sound or physical movement. It will be a matter of gazing at one object or repeating some sound or movement. In every case, what is involved is the focus on a single source of stimulation.

For this exercise, get into a comfortable sitting position. If you are at ease with your legs tailor-fashion or in a modified lotus posture, fine. If not, then sit comfortably in a chair with your feet flat on the floor, your legs and arms uncrossed and not touching. This exercise can be done anywhere, even on public transportation commuting to your job. But it really is much more beneficial to give yourself a private time and place to do it.

Allow the body to become totally relaxed and completely still. You may want to mentally go over your body, directing any pockets of tension that you find to just relax and let go.

The eyes are closed and remain closed throughout. Next, choose a phrase or sound that you like. Almost any neutral sound or phrase will work. You might like to choose one that has special meaning for you, or you might prefer a sound that has no meaning if you feel that it will distract you less. I like to use the sound *so* (which means "I am" in Sanskrit) on the inhalation and the sound *hum* (which means "that") on the exhalation. But feel free to choose any sound or sounds that are pleasing to you.

Remain quietly breathing in and out. Have your breaths be steady, regular. Mentally repeat the sound or phrase that you have chosen in a calm though concentrated way. Do not work at this. Although concentration is not easy, there is no *effort* involved. Just breathe in and out and repeat the sound. If thoughts come, notice them, dismiss them and return calmly to the sound. Even a few moments of this meditation exercise can be valuable, but the best plan is to consider ten minutes as a minimum amount of time to spend with it. Twenty minutes would be even better.

Concentration With the Eye: For this you choose any object that pleases your eyes. You might choose a flower, a vase, a design that you like. Place the object in front of you in such a way that you can look at it easily without straining. Sit comfortably and fix your eyes on the object you have chosen and keep them there. Keep your attention solely on the object, noticing its form and color. Consider every aspect of it and it alone. Do not think about anything else. You will find that your mind will wander. Just firmly and gently bring it back to the object. This is a demanding exercise and should not be continued for more than two or three minutes. Because of the brief moments necessary to achieve results with this method, you may use it any time that you find yourself with a few spare moments. No matter where you are, you simply fix your eyes on a single point and attempt to hold your mind on this point.

Candle Concentration: This technique combines external and internal concentration. Sit comfortably with a lighted candle placed in front of you at such a distance that you do not have to strain to see it (usually about three feet from you). Relax and gaze directly into the flame of the candle. Do not strain.

Blink as necessary. But keep gazing at the flame for about two minutes. Then close your eyes, placing your hands in such a way that the palms are lightly pressed against your eyelids. You will discover that the image of the candle is retained when you close your eyes. Concentrate, focus. Keep the image of the candle before you. Do not allow it to wander or disappear. If it does, simply look for it (while keeping the eyes closed). If your mind wanders, simply bring it firmly back to the image of the flame. Keep the palms pressed against the eyelids in this manner for another two minutes. In other words, the entire process takes about four minutes. After a while you will be able to hold the image of the candle steady with your eyes closed.

Concentration With Sound: There are two approaches that are valuable in this area. For both you will need a quiet, private place because of their subtlety.

The first is to choose an external sound to focus on. This could be some music that you like or it could be the sound of a bird or a river or the wind. The method used is to sit absolutely still with the eyes closed and to focus entirely on that one auditory source of stimulation for three or four minutes. This is very difficult to do. You have to be on guard against the images that will come to your mind associated with the sound as well as the random thoughts. Again, when you find that your mind has wandered, you must bring it back to the sound. After a while you should be able to lose the concept of you being there listening to the sound. You may find moments during which the sound seems to flow through you beyond any understanding or hearing that you have experienced before.

The second form of concentration with sound is one in which you close your eyes and attempt to hear the sound that is within your own ear. This is somewhat similar to the sound that you hear when you place a seashell next to your ear. This exercise requires that you completely withdraw from any external stimulation. You will find that the sound seems to disappear as soon as any thought comes to mind or other sounds intrude. Simply bring it back. Concentrate for three to five minutes.

Concentration With the Voice: For this, we will use the sound *om,* a Yogic incantation used for centuries. With your eyes closed, slowly inhale deeply and—using about half of the breath—very slowly sound the letter "O." The sound should be low and steady. Next, close your mouth and sound the letter "M." Feel the vibrations throughout your head and body. Concentrate totally on the sound, immerse yourself in it, become it. When all the breath has been used, inhale without pause and repeat at least seven times. Keep your voice low and steady throughout.

Concentration With the Breath: I will describe two techniques here. The first is alternate-nostril breathing. In this method, the flow of the breath is controlled by alternately stopping your nostrils in such a way that you inhale for a period of time, retain the breath for a few moments, and exhale slowly.

Sit comfortably with the spine erect, the eyes closed. Place your right elbow lightly against your right side, your right hand in front of your face with the palm facing you. The middle two fingers are bent inward, and the thumb and end two fingers are free to be placed over either nostril. (See the illustration.) There is no tension. The hand remains relaxed.

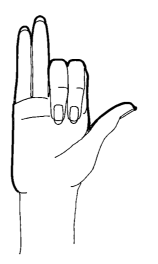

You begin by exhaling deeply through both nostrils. Now press your thumb against one nostril, thus closing it off. The other nostril remains open. Inhale slowly and deeply through the open nostril. Now close off this nostril with the two end fingers. This closes off both nostrils. Hold for a few moments, retaining the breath with the nostrils closed. Now remove your thumb from the nostril that it has closed and slowly exhale through this nostril. Immediately and without pause, inhale through this open nostril. Now close this nostril off as you retain the breath and then slowly exhale through the alternate nostril. See if you can inhale and exhale for an amount of time that is double the time that you retain the breath. In other words, you might inhale for a slow count of eight, retain the breath for a count of four, and exhale again for a count of eight.

After you have done five rounds of this alternate-nostril breathing, place your hand in your lap and remain quiet for a few moments with your eyes closed.

The second form of concentration with the breath is loosely based on a technique used in Kundalini Yoga. In this exercise, you sit quietly with your eyes closed, your spine erect. After a deep inhalation through both nostrils, you hold the breath for a period of time. The length of time varies with the practitioner. It should be long enough to be challenging, yet short enough so that the exhalation of breath remains under your control. That is, you do not gasp for breath. You inhale, hold the breath (say for a slow count of ten) and slowly exhale. Then inhale, hold the breath . . . and exhale—and so on for several minutes. This is a very powerful exercise, and if done for longer periods of time, its effects are cumulative.

The exercises described in this chapter seem almost naïve in their simplicity, and the most difficult achievement for the practitioner will be keeping at them. My suggestion would be to keep before you the image of how you feel after using one of the techniques. Again, understanding them is not what this is about. You must experience them.

> The traditional esoteric psychologies are, in their essence, neither deliberately exotic and incomprehensible nor irrelevent to our concerns. They constitute important new input for modern scientific psychology, about an area of inquiry and an area of the mind which has largely been ignored and forgotten in contemporary culture and psychology.[13]

Chapter 6

——◄♦►——

Memory

A friend of mine has a phone-answering machine. When she first purchased it, she was aware that her primary difficulty would probably be that she would forget to turn it on as she left the house. Having considered this problem, she discovered what is—for her—a nearly foolproof system: She knows that she will not leave home without having her keys in hand, and she has decided always to place her keys on top of her answering machine; therefore, when she reaches for her keys, she must remember to turn on her machine. At the same time, the first thing that she does upon entering the house is to place her keys on top of the machine; in that way she remembers to pick up her messages, and she sets up the system to work the next time.

This story nicely illustrates many of the main points that will be covered in this chapter. It is not my intention here to deal with problems of memory stemming from senility or disease, or to duplicate what can be learned in a memory course or popular memory book. Although I will discuss a few of the most helpful techniques, my main objective will be to discuss the memory improvement that is possible for any average individual and to point out the relationship between a conscious use of the memory apparatus and the resultant improvement in intelligence.

Before discussing my friend with the phone-answering device, it might be helpful to define terms. What is memory anyway? The dictionary defines it as "the general function of reviving or reliving past experience, with more or less definite realization that the present experience is a revival. Four distinct phases of memory have been recognized: (a) memorizing or learning, (b) retention, (c) recall, (d) recognition."[1]

In other words, memory is inextricably tied to learning; that is, the way that you demonstrate that you have learned something is by remembering it. And, since learning is tied similarly to intelligence (you demonstrate intelligence by the amount and quality of material learned), then it follows that memory has an important relationship to intelligence. What this relationship is, however, is still not clear, since intelligence certainly entails more than memory. For example, some mental defectives have powerful abilities to memorize by rote, but they are unable to critically interpret what they memorize.

As far back as the nineteenth century, theories of memory have been proposed which identify two principal kinds of remembering. These have been labeled "short-term memory" and "long-term memory,"[2] and basically they correspond to our commonsense understanding of the difference between the kind of memory we employ when, for example, we look up a telephone number (which we retain for just as long as it takes us to dial) as opposed to a language that we haven't spoken in years and which, we may be surprised to find, is still retrievable under the right circumstances.

When we study "memory systems" or techniques, what we are basically concerning ourselves with is short-term memory because it is this aspect of memory that is under our conscious control. Of course the nature of the kind of information that we put into our short-term memory system determines what will eventually be transferred into the long-term system.

How do we exert that control? What kinds of processes can we use to remember? Obviously, different circumstances call for different methods. One very common method is that of "rehearsal," which is simply a repetition of the information that one wants to recall. If we have a context of additional, easily retrievable information, such as a mnemonic phrase or sentence, then we can utilize the process called "coding." Sometimes it is easier to recall information if it is seen in visual terms; this is called "imaging."

There are many such techniques available to us when we consciously set out to remember something. In other words, we select these control processes as a result of conscious decisions as to which would be the best to apply in a particular situation. This differs from what happens in the more-or-less permanent long-term memory system.

As a convenient short-cut to understanding the contrast between the two systems, you may want to think of the short-term store as containing conscious memories. In other words, this is where you go for help in problem-solving and decision-making. This is your working memory. Getting to the information in the long-term memory stores is much more complicated. It is a matter of choosing the probe that will activate the right information in the long-term store so that our search will produce the desired results.

As you know from your own experience, rehearsal is a very important control process. When we rehearse information, we retain it longer, and the longer information is retained in the short-term store, the more likely it is to be transferred to the long-term store (indicated by our ability to recall it at some later date).[3] We then come to the question: What makes us forget? What is the mechanism at work which leads to the loss of information? Judith Reitman, of the University of Michigan, conducted experiments which seem to suggest that what makes us forget certain information is the fact that we take in other, similar information. In other words, if you are consciously trying to retain something in the short-term store, material that is substantially different will not interfere with this retention, yet other similar material will cause a large loss.

When do we actually transfer information to the long-term system? This seems to happen mostly during or after we have rehearsed it. However, if it is important to us to be able to retrieve the information later, we should try to code it or associate it with other known material. This is because if we have no associations with which to activate our search, we will not easily have access to the long-term store. This is why rote rehearsal often fails.

Looked at from this point of view, any information that we

want is present in the long-term store. Forgetting, in this context, is simply a matter of not having the correct information at our disposal to probe into the retrieval process. In other words, since you will be dependent in the long run on how you set about remembering something now, it is definitely in your best interest to do it right the first time, to learn something thoroughly so that it can be retrievable later.

Obviously, the more that you can remember, the more intelligent you will feel and the more intelligent you will be perceived by others. Just as obviously, you cannot retain something that you haven't really learned to begin with. This is perhaps the single most important aspect of memory improvement: You must intend to remember, and you must thoroughly learn that which you wish to remember. What this actually means is that you must be consciously aware of the learned material, while in the process of learning it, in order to be able to recall it at a later time.

The axiom "Do it right the first time" is one that should become second nature to you. For example, you meet someone new and you don't quite hear his name, but you let it pass. How can you possibly remember it? Right now, decide that in the future you will *intend* to remember the names of the people you meet. Then, on meeting someone new, be sure that you really hear the name—if necessary, ask him to repeat it or even to spell it—then, closely observe the person you are speaking to. Look at him carefully, associating his particular name with his particular face. If you consciously do this, if you take the time to really meet him, you have a much better chance of remembering his name.

The same principle is involved in reading new material. If you cannot concentrate on it, then do something else, because you surely won't remember it. Take the split second necessary to carefully read and understand that difficult word you want to skim over; visualize as vividly as you can what is being discussed; make it meaningful to you; make mental associations of this new material with previously learned material. Do these things, and you have a good chance of being able to retain the new information.

William James says:

The more other facts a fact is associated with in the mind, the better possession of it our memory retains. Each of its associates becomes a hook to which it hangs, a means to fish it up by when sunk beneath the surface. Together they form a network of attachments by which it is woven into the entire tissue of our thought. The secret of a good memory is thus the secret of forming diverse and multiple associations with every fact we care to retain.[4]

In the example quoted at the beginning of this chapter, my friend's conscious intention was to remember to turn on her answering machine. She then made the association between the answering machine (new information) and the keys (previously learned information). Once she had connected them, she made it a point to always visualize them together; that is, when she needs her keys she sees her phone-answering machine, and when she thinks of the machine, she visualizes it with her keys on top.

The notion of doing something right the first time, of aiming for accuracy when first approaching new information, can equalize somewhat the difference that is apparent in the retention of motor learning versus verbal learning. Motor skills must usually be overlearned—i.e., done completely—to be done at all, and therefore more concentration is given to mastering a motor skill. Consider this from your own experience. Perhaps you used to type but haven't been near a typewriter for years. See how long it takes you to regain whatever degree of proficiency you once had. Or suppose you haven't been on a bicycle for a long time. How long do you think it would take you to be able to ride again? Experiments have proven that motor skills, once learned, are fairly easily regained.[5]

When you don't use a muscle, it atrophies; when you don't use a fact, you forget it. This is normal and unavoidable. What you can do is to set up conditions for yourself that make it less likely that you will forget that which is important to you.

One way to do this is to avoid overburdening the mind with trivia, or setting up conflicting situations for the mind to deal with. For example, if you must make an important phone call at a certain hour, then keeping that phone call on your mind will interfere with whatever else you are involved with until that time. Why not set an alarm clock for the desired hour? The point is not to keep testing your mind by expecting it to remember everything, but to organize things in advance so that your mind can deal with that which is happening now so that you will be able to easily retain it. If you have no difficulty remembering appointments, fine; if you do, get used to using a calendar. It's not cheating to create space in your life so that you can concentrate on the task at hand.

But what of the memory systems? Certainly some of the techniques developed can be helpful; however, it should be kept in mind that the use of elaborate memory systems may create a situation in which you are memorizing at the expense of real learning. By all means use any memory device that seems helpful to you. But at the same time, avoid those that are too complicated, as these will certainly interfere with true assimilation of material and, therefore, longer retention.[6]

Any way that you can impose order upon information that you wish to retain will help you to learn it thoroughly. For example, you might number items. It becomes easier to check yourself if you know that you have ten things to remember. Another way to impose order upon information would be to place items in alphabetical order. When learning a speech or reading a book, however, it will probably be more helpful if you pick out key words, phrases or ideas that can call forth entire sentences or concepts when they are invoked.

It might be helpful here to consider the concept of Gestalt psychology[7] in which the notion of "parts" with attributes of their own, independent of a "whole," is held to be misleading.

In other words, an adjuvant means to assimilate new material would be to recognize that "parts" derive their properties from their membership in a "whole" and, in fact, the whole is more than the sum of its parts would indicate.

What this means in practice is that you isolate out the key ideas in new material to be assimilated, keeping in mind their relationship to the whole speech or chapter or book. You then link these thoughts together, with the result that you have created your own shorthand version of the material at hand.

For example, suppose that you wanted to memorize Hamlet's famous soliloquy, "To be or not to be. . . ." Some of the key words and phrases that you might choose would be the following: "To be or not," "nobler in the mind," "take arms," "end the heartache," "a consummation," "what dreams may come," and so on. It doesn't really matter which ideas or phrases you decide are the key ones. The point is that once you have taken the time to carefully choose which phrases represent the key to the particular information that you want to remember, once you have thought about these phrases and thoroughly linked them, you will have assured yourself of a much easier task when it comes to fully learning and retaining the entire speech.

The key to using this device—and, in fact, any memory device—is to associate any new material to something that you already know. In Hamlet's soliloquy the ideas are not difficult to relate to our own experience. If, however, you come upon ideas whose meaning is somewhat diffuse for you, you must make it meaningful to you in some way if you want to be at all confident about being able to remember it.

Use any method you can when you make associations. Often, the more ludicrous an association is, the more likely you will be to retain the image. For example, say that you want to remember a list of unrelated items such as the following: plant, book, eggs, door, car, bandage, paper, closet, rug, etc. You might begin by visualizing a healthy *plant* growing out of a *book*. Your next step might be to see the book being used as a frying pan to cook *eggs*. Then you might see a fried egg used as a peephole in a *door*. The door, of course, would be driving a *car* which would be all *bandaged* up. It doesn't matter what image you choose. The only requirement is that you choose something silly enough to jar your mind out of its accustomed laziness and that you awaken your latent powers of visualization.

The total concept of the strength inherent in visualization is a fascinating one, and many of the suggestions in this book will deal specifically with developing your abilities in this area. For now it is sufficient for you to know, for example, that you can be almost certain of remembering to do something if you impress it firmly on your mind by repetition and clearly visualize yourself both remembering and doing it. You have to be firm in your intention to remember, and you have to have the confidence that you will. This confidence will grow as you experience that you can, in fact, remember.

One of the few specific memory techniques that I have found helpful is the use of basic memory pegs. The advantage of using peg words to memorize a list, for instance, lies in the fact that you do not have to go down a whole chain of items in order to locate the eighth item on the list.

To learn the ten most-used memory pegs, we will pair ten phonetic sounds with ten digits. Concentrate on the memory aids used to do this. They may seem silly, but they will greatly telescope the time it will take you to learn the memory pegs themselves.[8]

Digit	Phonetic Sound	Memory Aid
1	*t* or *d*	A typewritten small *t* has *one* downstroke.
2	*n*	A typewritten *n* has *two* downstrokes.
3	*m*	A typewritten *m* has three downstrokes
4	*r*	The word four ends with an *r*.
5	*l*	The *five* fingers, thumb out, form an *l*.
6	*j, sh, ch,* soft *g*	A 6 and a capital *J* are almost mirror images.
7	*k,* hard *c,* hard *g*	You can make a capital *K* with two 7s.
8	*f, v, ph*	An 8 and a handwritten *f* look similar.
9	*p* or *b*	A 9 and a *p* are mirror images.
0	*z, s,* soft *c*	The first sound in the word zero is *z*.

We are now ready to provide peg words for the ten digits. Since the peg words are based on the phonetic alphabet, they have a logic to them. And, as we now know, that which is logical or ordered, is easier to learn.

Digit	Letter	Peg Word
1	*t*	*Tea.* Picture a tall glass of iced tea.
2	*n*	*Noah.* Picture a man with a long gray beard.
3	*m*	*May.* Picture a calendar turned to that month.
4	*r*	*Ray.* Picture sun rays.
5	*l*	*Law.* Picture a policeman.
6	*j*	*Jaw.* Picture a man with a large jaw.
7	*k*	*Key.* Picture a large gold key.
8	*f*	*Fee.* Picture a price tag of a million dollars.
9	*b*	*Bay.* Picture land and water.
10	*t* and *s*	*Toes.* Picture ten toes.

Go over these until you feel comfortable with them. You should be able to match a random peg word with its number, or a number with its peg word, automatically. Once you know them fairly well, you are ready to use them as words on which to peg the items you wish to remember.

Let's take another look at the list of words we linked together before. The fifth item on that list was *car*. If you were to think of a policeman stopping a car, you would then remember that *car* was the *fifth* item on the list. Or take another word from the same list: *paper.* If you were to visualize a piece of paper being used as a key, you would remember that *paper* was the *seventh* item on the list. The images you come up with needn't be sensible in any way. They can make sense . . . as the idea of a policeman stopping a car. Or they can be totally absurd . . . like using paper as a key. What matters is that you have a clear mental picture of the two items together.

Even if you decide that the use of memory pegs is not for you, I suggest that you take the time to learn them. For our purposes, anything that you can do to exercise the mind will be to your advantage and will perhaps stimulate you to come up with solutions of your own.

There is nothing mysterious about remembering. In all of the examples given in this chapter, the same general principles are found to apply:

1. Make any material that you wish to remember significant to you in some way. Be interested in it or at least in the value of remembering it.

2. Give it your full attention. Be right the first time.

3. Understand it completely.

4. Have the intention and the confidence that you will remember it.

5. Associate it with other facts that you have already assimilated.

6. Break it down into key parts and—conversely—see smaller facts as parts of a larger whole.

7. Reinforce by repetition.

The simple fact is that you must assign special significance to something if you wish to remember it. You don't need to set aside time each day for memory training. What you must do is to give things your full attention *as they come up*. It takes only a fraction of time to do this. And if you focus completely on something—learn it, practice it and use it—then you will be able to remember it.

Chapter 7

Communication:
Getting the Information

As I have stressed in other chapters, an important aspect of the measurement of intelligence lies in how you are perceived by others. This, in turn, leads us directly to the subject of communication, since your ability to influence another's perception of you or of a situation depends, to a significant degree, on how well you can communicate your ideas.

Let us use, as our starting point in this discussion of communication, some of the definitions found in the *Dictionary of Psychological and Psychoanalytical Terms.*[1]

> Communication:
> Transmitting and receiving . . . information, signals or messages by means of gestures, words or other symbols, from one organism to another. . . .
> The total process whereby one system (a source) influences another system (a destination) by manipulation of the alternative signals carried in a channel connecting them.
> A high degree of dynamic dependence between two personal regions so that the changes in one bring about proportional changes in the other. . . .
> An attempt by one person to influence another whom he addresses in such a way as to reduce discrepancies between them.

Now that we have the basis for a working definition, let us examine it and see what we want to add for the purposes of this book, the aim of which is to help you increase your intelligence.

Communication begins with an idea that you have that you want to share with someone else. How did you get this idea? Through your experience of something, either active (you did something) or passive (you read or were told about something). Therefore, for our purposes, we will want to deal with your abilities in the area of getting the information.

Here we should briefly consider how well you read and how you approach a subject you want to master. Once again, it is not my intention here to duplicate material covered in other places, but rather to demonstrate to you how to apply general principles to increasing your intelligence.

Obviously, if you can read at a faster rate, you will have more information and will, therefore, be able to come to more intelligent conclusions. But before we consider the rate at which you read, let us look at how effectively you read.

The following general principles can be applied to most information-gathering material, and some of them are applicable to most kinds of reading. As will be apparent, however, some will not be desirable when approaching fiction-for-pleasure, for example.

The main point of these principles is that the way to achieve effective reading is not by studying more but by changing the quality of your study method.[2]

Method for Effective Study

1. At first, look at the material to be read in its entirety. Turn the pages of the entire segment as rapidly as you can, while you skim through the material. Try to get an *overview* of it. See if you can locate the major points. In most books you will find that these are indicated by centered headings or by bold-face type. Note subdivisions and summary paragraphs. See if you can identify the author's plan.

2. Now read the summary sections.

3. The next step is to recall from memory the major points of the chapter or segment. If, after your initial skimming, you are unable to recall the major points of the material, it will be an absolute waste of time for you to begin reading the segment proper. Keep repeating steps one through three until you have a firm idea of what the material deals with.

4. Now read any introductory material.

5. By this time, you should have a fairly accurate idea of what the author has in mind. Bring your own background and common sense to the subject and see what you already know about it. See if you can anticipate what is to come by locating what question it is the author is about to answer.

6. Now read the section until you come to the answer to that question. As you read, underline key words and ideas. If there are words that you don't understand, note their meaning in the margins.

7. When you have finished reading, take a moment to *recall from memory* the important parts of the section. Try not to refer back to the material; use your own words. Remember, if you cannot recall what you have read so far, it makes no sense at all to proceed to the next reading unit.

8. If you take the time to review what you have read—going over those points that you have underlined or noted in your margins, you will understand the material better and be able to retain it longer.

It cannot be emphasized too strongly that your willingness to approach new material with full concentration has a great deal to do with your ability to retain it. If you cannot give your full attention to the material at hand, then leave it until you can. As we have discussed before, you cannot analyze—much less remember—information half-learned.

Briefly, then, when you pick up a new book, look at it as a whole. Get an overview of it. Read the cover, the back jacket. Take a look at the introduction, the table of contents. In other words, see where the author intends to take you. This will give you a context within which to assemble individual facts. Remember, the more things some new fact can be associated with, the more likely you will be to remember it.

Next, read through for the main ideas. Don't get side-

tracked by details at first. The details will fall into place automatically once the main outline is clear.

Use the obvious: Headings, bold-face and italicized type are
there for a reason. Use judicious underlining and notes in the
margins.

Having done a thorough overview, you are truly ready to
read. You will know which sections should get most of your
attention, which are less important. You will have the parameters of a whole picture into which you can slug the details. You
will be in control of the material.

We are now ready to consider the question of speed. It has
been noticed that people who are naturally fast readers have
several reading habits in common: They all read in a downward direction as well as in the usual left to right direction;
they seem to absorb whole areas of a page rather than getting
stuck on individual words; and they adjust their speed depending on the kind of material they are reading.

There are specific techniques that you can use to increase
your reading speed. But since you will be reading in a new
way, it should be noted that certain words will be taking on
slightly different connotations. In order to avoid confusion,
let us take a moment to define terms.

First of all, when you are reading to increase speed you
will be reading for *adequate comprehension* as opposed to total
comprehension. In other words, you must recognize at the
outset that you will be aiming for that amount of comprehension that is sufficient to meet your needs and purposes
of the moment.

Practice, in this context, means moving the eyes over the
page at speeds beyond which you can achieve satisfactory
comprehension. Let me emphasize that in order to stabilize
reading at increased speeds, you will have to practice at levels
beyond satisfactory comprehension.

When you practice, often you will want to time yourself and
compute your rate of speed. There is an easy way to do this.
First you find the average words per page in this manner:

1. Count the number of words on three full lines.

2. Divide this total by three to find the average words per
line.

3. Now count the number of lines on a full page.

4. Multiply (2) by (3) to get the average words per page.

Now, here is how to find the average words per minute that you are reading:

1. Multiply the number of words per page by the number of pages read.

2. Divide the total by the number of minutes you've been reading.

When reading with this method, you must learn to use the hand as a pacer. The point of using the hand is to provide a guide for the eye, to keep the eye from getting bogged down. By learning to read quickly in a downward motion on the page—in addition to the left-to-right motion—you will learn to avoid the intermediate step of the reader who says or thinks or hears the sounds of words as he reads them.

In the following section, I will describe some hand movements. For the moment, just read through the section; you will have a chance to practice the movements in another section. Note that these are suggested hand movements that have been found to be helpful. Once you become comfortable with these, you may choose to develop your own.

Hand Motions

1. Keeping your hand relaxed, place your index finger under your thumb. Now move your hand from left to right, line by line over the page. Try this with your palm up and then with your palm down to see which feels more comfortable for you. Move steadily and rapidly.

2. This is the same as (1), except that your hand comes off the page at about the middle of each line. Try to see everything on the page, but do not be concerned about understanding everything.

3. *The Straight "L":* Keep your hand relaxed and your palm down. Come straight across the page under the first line. Now, form a loop upwards and come down about three lines. Then move up and across the page under the line. (See the illustration.)

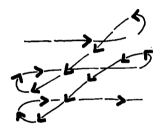

4. *The Slanted "L"*: This is a slightly downhill left-to-right motion that forms an "L" shape. The cross-over is important because it enables you to get another look at the material you've just seen.

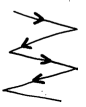

5. *The Zigzag:* This motion is especially good for newspaper reading. In the Zigzag, you form a "Z" shape over the material.

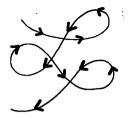

6. *The Sloppy "S"*: This is good for fiction reading.

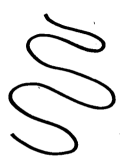

You are now ready to begin your practice. Remember to maintain a steady, easy motion with each exercise.

To do the following exercises, set aside an area at a table or desk with good lighting. In other words, although later you will be able to read with this method in your favorite lounge chair, it would be better at first to break your old habits by approaching this new method in a businesslike manner.

Page Turn: How silly, you say. I already know how to turn pages. You'd be surprised to learn, however, how much time is lost in brief awkwardness. So take some time now and practice turning pages as quickly as you can. As you do this, use your hand as a pacer, going straight down the center of each page, your eyes following your hand. Try to see each page, but do not attempt to read or comprehend what you see. Just take each page in quickly. Aim to go as rapidly as you can—and at a steady, rhythmical rate.

Hand Motions: Using each of the hand motions, repeat the previous exercise. You are seeing each page, but you are not attempting to comprehend. This is to familiarize yourself with the hand motions. Take the time to become comfortable with them.

You are now ready to practice reading at increased speeds. Remember that you will have to push your practice rates up beyond comprehension. The way that you then stabilize your new speed is to repeat the material while decreasing the time. Practice your hand motions until they are smooth and rhythmical. Change the hand motions every once in a while so that you're eyes don't habituate.

As we discussed in the section on studying effectively, your overview of the material is of vital importance to your comprehension. Never omit this preview of material to be read. Your approach to the reading of new material should be consistent: a *preview* or *overview* as discussed before, coupled with a period of *recall* for the main ideas. You then *read* the section for adequate comprehension, following this with another period of *recall.* Then you quickly go over the material again, in a *postview,* following this with another period of *recall.* This may seem like a lot of going over the same material, but if you follow these instructions you will be reading faster, understanding more and, even more important, retaining more.

When you first approach the material, rapidly practicing through it, remember that "practice" in this context means going above your comprehension levels. You do not "dig" for facts at this time, but instead remain open to impressions, mood and atmosphere.

READING DRILL

1. Mark off a ten-page section. Using the first hand motion described, practice these ten pages. Now practice the same section with the same hand motion at a faster rate. Next, write a brief summary of what you believe this section to be about.

Now repeat these steps with the next ten-page section; and again with a third ten-page section; and again with a fourth ten-page section. You have now previewed forty pages and are ready to read.

2. Read the first ten-page section as quickly as you can using the Straight "L" or the Slanted "L" hand motion.

3. Now postview this section. This is similar to what you did in your preview except that now you are going over material instead of approaching new material. Remember that in a postview you move rapidly. See if you can do this in thirty seconds. When you are finished, add to your written summary.

4. Repeat these steps with the other ten-page sections.

5. Now, read through all the material as rapidly as you can. You are reading now for adequate comprehension. Use any comfortable hand motion and remember to maintain speed.

6. Compute your words per minute.

As you become more comfortable with the hand motions, you will begin to see which are more helpful for which parts of the drill. Each time that you do this drill, use a new forty-page unit.

READING DRILL

1. Using the Straight "L" hand motion, read a short paragraph in about two seconds.
2. Write a brief summary of the paragraph on a piece of scratch paper.
3. Reread the paragraph quickly, using the same hand motion. In this way you check on comprehension and recall and you can begin to develop eye-mind reassurance.
4. Repeat this practice with the different hand motions on new material.

Earlier in this chapter, when we discussed study habits, you were instructed to skim in your initial overview of the material. When you learn to read with the method we have been discussing, there is this difference: You must try to take in everything on the page. In other words, *do not skim.* What I mean is that although you are going at beyond your ability to get adequate comprehension, you still *see* each page totally. This is true all the way through: During your initial preview or overview of the material; when you practice each section; and when you finally read.

What you will be doing is allowing the words to come into your brain without being fixated on each word or group of words as you go along. Until you have experienced that, in fact, it is possible to understand and recall material read in this way, you may not believe that you can do this. The proof will lie in your ability to recall what you have read.

When you *recall,* what you are doing is writing or telling or thinking in your own words what you have seen, experienced or read. This represents the ultimate test of comprehension. When you set out to recall what you have read, think in terms of key ideas and words from which you can expand. Don't get lost in story lines. A helpful plan is to diagram your recall on a separate sheet of paper.

Two points should be noted here. First, it is not unusual to have delayed recalls—ones that develop some time after the reading. You may "go blank" at first and then start remembering. A quick look at the material will often start the chain reaction of recall.

Second, recalling develops only through practice. It is a

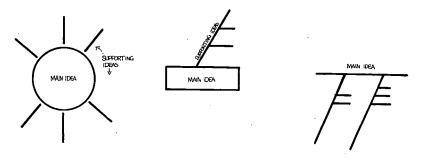

separate skill from the reading process and requires separate practice to develop.

READING DRILL

[Note: The use of a kitchen timer will free
you so that you can fully concentrate on
the drill.]
1. Preview about forty pages in three minutes.
2. Read through from the beginning for adequate comprehension. Remember that reading always means using your hand as a pacer. Go as rapidly as you can for about five minutes.
3. Now compute your words per minute and record this as your "low" rate.
4. Using a separate sheet of paper, recall for one or two minutes. Remember to concern yourself with main ideas, key points.
5. Now set up four sections, using markers. Each section should be equal to the amount read in (2) of this drill.
6. In each section, one at a time:
   a. Overview the section in about one and a half minutes.
   b. Read the section in three minutes.
   c. Postview the section in one minute.
   d. Recall the section taking one to two minutes.
7. Now, in new material:
   a. Overview for one minute. Go as rapidly as you possibly can.
   b. Read for adequate comprehension for five minutes as rapidly as possible.

c. Postview what you have just read taking about half a minute.

d. Now compute your words per minute using five minutes as your total time and record this as your "high" rate.

e. Using a separate sheet of paper, recall the material for one or two minutes.

Reading is thinking with an aid. The aid is the printed page containing the symbols that act as stimuli for the mind. These symbols trigger the mind to think along specific lines.

To improve your reading, you must sharpen your thinking. Learning to read generally down the page is mentally challenging. It involves learning and using new patterns of perceiving. In order to break your accustomed ways of doing this, you need to use your hand as a pacer—always.

As you train yourself to move generally down the page, remember to reach for seeing all of the print on the page. Do not skim. You will learn to get above the print and view it as though from an airplane viewing a city below. As you move down the page, see whole areas of print. Do not make your eyes follow each motion of the hand slavishly, but let them go where they will.

Look for total concepts within which to become aware of details. You will discover that you hang on to individual words or phrases less and less, that you begin to see words in groups. Allow all the words to come in rapidly. Do not stop and consider them individually. Reading this way, words come in so fast that we do not have time to evaluate them until they have become part of a whole idea. Thus, you become more dependent upon feeling, atmosphere, mood. You become part of the story, thinking with the author. Therefore, you will usually receive from the reading more vivid and lasting impressions.

Remember, you must continue to spend some time regularly practice-reading above comprehension-level speed, then dropping back to an improved comprehension level.

Theoretically, it would be ideal to do all of your reading this way. My experience, however, has been that there is some material that I absolutely do not want to read at high speeds. The point of learning this or any other method is not to follow it mechanically, but to have it at your disposal to use or not as you see fit.

So practice to raise your reading level, and then adjust your speed as you wish for different material. As you become more and more able to relax while remaining alert, you will find that you are becoming a visual, rather than a vocal reader.

Chapter 8

Communication:
Getting Ideas Across

Now that you know how to go about getting the information, we are ready to look at the next major aspect of communication, which has to do with getting your ideas across. Here we should consider both your knowledge of words and the way you approach the process of communication itself.

Words are the medium through which we communicate. They are our tools, and we must be completely at ease with them if we wish to express our desires accurately, communicate our feelings persuasively and influence others. If this does not sufficiently motivate you, you should know that research indicates that when you function with a limited vocabulary, you limit your chances of success.

For example, it was found that out of 100 men whose vocabulary skills were tested, all of those who were in the upper 10 percent had succeeded in achieving executive positions five years later, while none of the men who had tested in the lower 25 percent held executive positions.[1]

People perceive you as intelligent and therefore capable of leadership when you make use of an extensive vocabulary. Then, too, words add amazingly to your power to think. So make it your intention to increase your working vocabulary. There are simple ways you can do this. But first, a general warning: Having more words at your disposal means being able to choose the specific words that you need; it is not a matter of using long or complicated words where simpler ones will do. Words are there to facilitate your ability to communicate and to enable you to express your thoughts accurately, not to conceal what you mean. Your aim should always be for clarity and simplicity. At the same time, however, you should realize that one precise word can often replace an entire phrase.

The best way to get at the meaning of a new word is to try and see it first in the context in which it is used. Just as when reading for speed you were instructed to reach for the whole and not get bogged down in details, so with an unfamiliar word, see it first in its surroundings. Try to deduce the meaning of the unfamiliar from the overall implications of the material.

For many words this process will suffice. But when you come upon a word that you want to know thoroughly, you will have to take more time with it. As you can see, you will not be able to fully combine your speedreading with vocabulary building. However, as you may have realized already, many of the techniques learned in memory training can easily be applied to the study of language.

A new word will be assimilated smoothly if you take the fraction of time necessary to give it your full attention, understand it completely, have the intention that you will remember it, associate it with other facts that you have already assimilated and reinforce by repetition.

You will have to take a moment to make a new word your own. Say it aloud. If you are not comfortable pronouncing it, you certainly won't be at ease using it. Spell it. Write it down. Think of synonyms and antonyms for it. In this way the meaning of a new word will gradually become clear to you in a thorough way. The next step is to try and define the new word using your own words.

This is a very difficult thing to do. Consider, for example, how you would define an abstraction like "love" to someone who had never experienced it. What about a color? What does "green" mean? By attempting to put a new word into concrete individual terms, you will have focused your attention on it, concentrating with intensity and without distraction on it. This will make that word clear for you in a more complete way that anything else could have done.

Do not expect your definitions to match the language in a dictionary. That is not the point. What you are after is covering approximately and substantially the same ground. When you can define a word in your own words, you will feel confident about using it.

An important point to notice is that you are not being encouraged to use jargon or unnecessarily complicated language. What you are aiming for is clarity. Having the accurate word at your disposal can save you much wasted effort, but trying to be sophisticated will just lead to pretentiousness. Once again, it is a matter of having the tools ready when you want them.

Once you begin to see clearly the words you previously skimmed over, you will realize that many words have the same Greek and Latin roots. It doesn't take much effort to familiarize yourself with these, and it's an effort that will put you way ahead when you come up against an unknown word.

Here are some of the more common roots. Take the time to learn them.

1. *Monos* (Greek), "one," as in monogamy and monotheism.

2. *Gamos* (Greek), "marriage," as in monogamy, bigamy, misogamy and polygamy.

3. *Bis* (Latin), "twice" or "two," as in bigamy and bicuspid.

4. *Polys* (Greek), "many," as in polygamy and polyglot.

5. *Misein* (Greek), "to hate," as in misogamy and misanthropy.

6. *Theos* (Greek), "god," as in monotheism, bitheism and polytheism.

7. *Glotta* (Greek), "tongue," as in polyglot.

8. *Anthropos* (Greek), "man," as in misanthropy.

9. *Logos* (Greek), "knowledge, "study," as in theology.

10. *Philein* (Greek), "to love," as in philanthopist.

Become aware of the power of words. Choose verbs and adjectives that will enhance and enrich your thoughts. If all this seems like a lot of work, remember that it will take only a few moments to do it right the first time and make an unfamiliar word your property. And the reward includes the elimination of that vaguely uncomfortable feeling that is inevitable when you come up against a word that you know you've looked up in the dictionary before and still do not know the precise meaning of.

Let's look now at what happens during the process of communication. Communication should be a fairly mechanical affair during which one person gets a message that another sends. What complicates the process is that while the first person is using words to convey his message, the rest of his behavior is also communicating a message. His attitude towards what he is saying, in addition to how he feels about himself as well as the other person—all will influence how he sends his message. Then, too, how his message is received will be determined to some extent by the other person's feelings and attitudes.

What complicates the process even further is that both people may be only subliminally—or not at all—aware that they are communicating messages not intended. If this is something that is not immediately apparent to you, you can test it for yourself by saying a simple phrase different ways. For example, try saying the words "I am not angry" in a variety of ways. It should be obvious that many different messages can be sent with the same word content.

When we consider interpersonal communication, we have to realize that talking to another person has dynamic implications—each person's reactions influencing the other's future reactions.

In looking at the possibilities for improving your ability to communicate with others, what we are after is not a matter of locating a "right" way to communicate. The point is to discover if you are communicating what you intend to communicate. What are the actual consequences of your communication? What you should aim towards is a situation in which all of your behavior (words, actions, body movement) is communicating the same message. You have to become sensitive enough to notice if your words and actions are consistent with your feelings or going against them.

One of the most effective ways available for improving communication is the use of a feedback mechanism. It can be very helpful if another tells us what he heard us say (as opposed to what we thought we said) and how he felt about what we said. We are then in a good position to decide if we should modify our methods of communication. Remember, what is involved here is the notion of congruence—of sending the message you thought you sent.

There are different ways of providing feedback, and it may be helpful here to note certain characteristics that constructive feedback has:

First, constructive feedback steers clear of evaluating; it describes. When behavior is described rather than judged, the need for defensive reaction is greatly reduced.

Second, constructive feedback is specific. General statements about some form of behavior do not provide an opportunity for specific, positive reactions.

Third, constructive feedback is directed at behavior that can be controlled. It is very frustrating to be reminded of failings over which one has no control.

Fourth, if possible, it is timed so that the receiver is open to it; ideally, it is requested instead of being imposed.

Fifth, it is checked for accuracy. Very often the receiver of feedback does not get the message accurately. One way of making sure that this does not happen is to have the receiver put the feedback message into his own words and see if the giver agrees that this is the message that he sent.

The nature of feedback would seem to dictate the presence of another person, and certainly another—outside—eye can be enormously helpful when we wish to test our perceptions. But there are constructive steps we can take unilaterally to sharpen our awareness of how we communicate. Because these exercises are aimed at deepening your self-awareness, they will also—although indirectly—help in your communication with others. This is because often our difficulties in communication begin as a result of our insensitivity and "out-of-touch-ness" with ourselves. Once again, these exercises work, but even if they didn't, just by doing them you will be expanding your mental capabilities.

1. Find a comfortable—but not collapsed—position. It is best if your hands are not touching and your legs are uncrossed. Close your eyes.

Now, bring your attention to your body. Go over your body mentally and locate any sensations that are there. Do not try to increase or decrease what you find. Just note any sensation that you feel, describe it to yourself, and then locate another sensation. There is nothing to fix and you don't have to finish anything.

Next, *choose* for those bodily sensations to be there. In other words, no matter what you find, choose that. This could be a tingling in your fingers, a pain in your back, a feeling of energy—whatever. Keep your evaluations of "good" and "bad" out of what you find in your body. Locate the sensations, describe them—and *choose* for them to be there.

Now let your attention leave your body and center on your emotions. What are you feeling right now? Sad? Happy? Angry? Don't try to manipulate your feelings into what you think you *should* feel. Just see how it is with you right now, and choose that. Really feel that feeling, emote that emotion. If you find that your feelings change simply as a result of looking at them, what emotions take their place? Choose *them.*

All right, let go of your emotions. This doesn't mean that you should not have your emotions. It just means that you somewhat detach from them, that you can have them or not and you can bring your attention to your attitude.

What position are you coming from right now? What is your attitude toward things? Choose that. Really take that position. Really come from that point of view.

Now, let your attitude go. This doesn't mean that you shouldn't have an attitude. It simply means that you aren't fixed in having one. That you can have it or not.

Last, ask yourself what is really going on with you right now. As you answer this question, choose for that to be going on. Again—what is going on with you right now? Perhaps the same thing. Choose that. If you find your answer has changed, take a look at the answer that comes up for you and choose that.

Take whatever comes to you in this exercise no matter how illogical it might seem. Just look at how things are for you at *this precise moment,* and choose that.

There is absolutely no way to *understand* this exercise. The rational "this . . . and then this . . . and then this" does not come close to explaining the experience of *doing* it. So reread the instructions, and *experience* the exercise.

2. Stand sideways in front of a full-length mirror. Relax completely and, without consulting the mirror, assume the position that you usually do when standing and talking to someone. It is foolish to cheat and take a "good posture" position.

Once you are certain that this is your habitual pose, take a look in the mirror. Do not change your position. Really look at how you look when you believe you are making a good impression on another.

3. This is the same as the previous exercise except that you take a seated position still facing profile to the mirror. Remember, do not change the position you have assumed. Look at it.

4. Ideally you should have a tape recorder for this exercise. If not, you can still find one of those machines in the five-and-dime where you can make a short recording of your voice. Choose something that you feel very comfortable with to read. Do not try to correct your speech in any way. The point is to have an accurate record of how you actually sound.

Listen to the tape or record. Then put it away for a few days, then listen to it again. Try simply to listen. Is that how you thought you sounded?

5. Refer to the chapter on Meditation, and do the exercise called "The Witness." Remember not to judge what you see as you witness exactly what you are doing. You are simply noticing that you are doing such and such, and then you are doing such and such, and then you are doing such and such.

6. As you talk to someone else, as you go about your daily activities, take a moment to notice your facial expressions, your hand motions, whether you sit quietly or fidget, etc. See if you can let go of anything extraneous to your just being there. See how close you can come to just being there without anything added. This sounds simple. It can be incredibly difficult to achieve.

These exercises will subtly change your perception of yourself. It is not my purpose here to tell you how you *should* look or sound. Once again, it is a question of *congruence.* Are you projecting what you think you are? What you do with the self-awareness you gain from doing these exercises is completely up to you.

Chapter 9

Communication:
Getting Another's Ideas

The last major component of communication that we will consider has to do with your willingness to get what another person is trying to communicate to you. Here we will want to look at what is involved in listening, as well as the idea of accepting another's viewpoint as being valid. We will also discuss the important distinction between acceptance and agreement.

What actually happens when we do what we habitually call listening to another? Usually we form a judgment or an evaluation of what the other is saying. We either approve or disapprove of his statement or position.

Consider this in reference to your own experience. If you objectively look at your reactions to another, you will find that your first reaction is almost invariably an evaluation of what has been said from your own point of view and your personal frame of reference.

Of course, whenever feelings and emotions come into play, this natural tendency toward evaluation is magnified many times, and when two people are coming exclusively from their own frames of reference, it is impossible for any genuine communication to take place. What you then have is two totally separate messages which miss each other. In such a case, both sides in the missed communication are, in fact, talking about different things.

Take a moment here and look into your own experience. As supposedly rational human beings, we tend to think that we act logically and that, in fact, the process of communication is a logical one. We assume that words in themselves—apart from the people involved—have meaning. And we assume that the purpose of an interaction between people is for one person to come to agree with the other. Take a moment to consider your last missed communication. If you are like most people, you won't have to look far to come up with one. Can you sense that you and the other person were, however subtly, really talking about two different things?

Well, what can be done about this? How do you get around the tendency to evaluate? One way is by being willing to re-create exactly how it is for the other person. This means actually trying to see the idea from his point of view, to sense how he feels about it, to put yourself in his frame of reference. This is, in practice, an incredibly difficult thing to achieve because it means being so clear about what it is precisely that the other person means that you could summarize his thoughts and feelings for him.

Of course, if you really do listen in this manner, you are taking a risk. If you are genuinely willing to enter another's private world and see how things appear from his point of view—without adding any evaluations from yours—you run the risk of being changed yourself. You might find that you are influenced in your attitudes. You might end up seeing things his way.

If you are willing to take that risk, at least on some level, then you can experiment with this theory yourself. You can, of course, enlist the cooperation of the person you are trying to communicate with. But you can approach the process obliquely. The next time you sense that something is going wrong in a communication, instead of trying to hammer home your point or beginning to explain it for the umpteenth time, try to summarize *his* point instead—and to his satisfaction. Repeat what the other person said. Restate it in your own words. Really try to understand his point of view. Then see for yourself what happens to the exchange. See what happens to the final result. When you see it his way, you may find that your own comments have to be revised. In addition, you may discover the emotion going out of the discussion and the differences between you being reduced. The discussion, at that point, will turn into something rational and understandable.

Another exercise that you can practice in the presence of another but without advising the other of what you are doing, is simply to talk less and listen more. Probably one of the most common approaches to communication is that two people take turns talking, each barely waiting until the other has stopped to get in what he wants to say. If you make a conscious effort to listen, to genuinely consider what another is saying, you will be on the road to actually hearing what is being said.

An interesting by-product of this is that the person you are talking to will pick up the cue from your attitude—remember that all behavior is part of communication—and will feel better about talking to you as he begins to feel that you respect him and what he believes. Therefore, he will be more likely to be receptive to what you do eventually say.

An important point to notice is that successful communication is not a matter of one person coming around to accept what the other person has said. Successful communication occurs when both people are free to express feelings and ideas in an atmosphere in which they will be respected. In successful communication there is a willingness to admit the existence of differences.

And now we come to the subtle, but dangerously important distinction between acceptance and agreement. Often during a lecture, someone in the audience will bring up the Holocaust as an indisputable argument against acceptance of another's ideas. Let me explain here the contrast between acceptance and agreement, using Nazi Germany as my example.

Obviously, many Germans supported the rise of the Third Reich or it wouldn't have gained the power that it did. Of those who were antagonistic towards its aims, however, there were those who saw what was happening and refused to believe that the "ridiculous house painter" would, in fact, gain the power to destroy millions. There were others who understood only too well and who railed against fate and talked of the injustice of the world. And there were others who accepted the reality—however ugly they deemed it—of that milieu. Some of these fled their homeland; some of them fought in the Underground or in whatever ways were open to them.

It is not my purpose here to demonstrate all the options available to the German people facing the rise of Hitler. But I believe that even this superficial description of that complex period of history serves to make the point that when you accurately *get* what another is saying you are free to act upon your new knowledge. Also, I have used this extreme example to show conclusively that you do not have to agree with someone to truly understand where he is coming from. Agreement and disagreement should be left out of the communication process proper. They come later, after you are sure that you completely understand another's message.

In the last three chapters, we have looked at three major aspects of communication. I have called these: getting the information, getting ideas across and getting another's ideas. You can improve interpersonal communication, influence another's perception of you and therefore increase your intelligence. To do this, you must have a clear idea of something that you want to share; you must have the tools at hand so that you can truly re-create your experience vividly; and you must be willing to re-create another person's experience as well.

Chapter 10

Creative Imagination

In a recent experiment, three groups of students were measured in reference to improvement in their basketball game. The first group was given systematic instruction and practice over a period of time; the second group did not practice physically, but was instead instructed in mental practice and given time to do that; the third group, used as a control, was given no instruction of any kind.

At the end of the prescribed time, all three groups' abilities were measured. The first and second groups, as expected, had improved more than the third; and, significantly, the second group—which had used only mental practice—had improved to about the same level as the first.

The mind is a powerful tool, and one that you can train to help you. The technique described in this chapter will aid you in sharpening your powers of imagination, visualization and concentration. By enabling you to experience vividly in your imagination, it will also free you to shed many of the considerations that place limits on your intelligence. It is fairly obvious, after all, that you cannot do things that you are convinced are beyond you. The technique discussed here will demonstrate ways of getting beyond your concept of yourself, thereby opening up new possibilities of acting and being to you.

It is important to note, however, that it is not necessary that you "believe" in any magic properties of this exercise. Even if it did not work—which it does—it would still serve the purpose of sharpening your mental skills and, therefore, of tapping into a more powerful intelligence.

Since it will be necessary to practice visualizing something, I suggest that you use your own goals. Again, don't concern yourself with whether the technique will work; just practice and see what happens. Begin by taking a moment to consider some of the things that you would like to experience in your life. It is important that you actually write them down, take them out of the vague atmosphere of fantasy and put them into tangible form. You cannot bring a plan to fruition until you have a plan; you cannot realize a goal until you have made that goal vivid and clear to yourself, until you begin to consider it possible right now. Do it.

I cannot emphasize enough the importance of making your list as concrete as possible. To say that you desire insight or some other intangible thing is to avoid facing the issue; what is necessary here is that you specify some solid reality that you would like to see in your world. Have some long-term goals, but include short-term goals as well.

What we will be doing is utilizing imagination and visualization in order to enable you to capture the state of feeling that you would have if your dreams were a reality.

But what, exactly, is imagination? For our purposes, imagination will be differentiated from daydreaming and fancy. Imagination[1] can mean the representation of future events, especially of the goal sought (goal image), or of the movements (movement image) needed to achieve the goal. Constructive or creative imagination, then, is an intentional recombining of images, either for its own sake or as a plan for action. This differs from fanciful imagination, in which the subject remains relatively passive and the recombining of portions from past experience seems to proceed without volition, as in dreams, daydreams and the imaginings of delusion and hallucination. It also differs from memory imagination (memory images), the more or less complete representation of a formerly experienced object or event, coupled with the recognition that it does represent a past actually experienced.

The technique that will be described here deals with the use of creative imagination. Not—as in daydream—imagination as an escape from reality, but imagination used for the purpose of creating a new reality.

The practice of the technique itself is not difficult. First, be sure that you are somewhere where you will not be disturbed. Take a few moments to relax the body using any technique that is comfortable for you. It can be helpful if you bring your attention to the different parts of your body and let a feeling of relaxation enter them. Take a few very deep breaths, holding the breath for several seconds before releasing it slowly; as you release the breath, allow all pressure and tension to seep away. Take your time and allow yourself to slip into that borderline state just below the level of consciousness.

This will be your opportunity to experience, in your imagination, how things would be if your dreams and goals were fulfilled. The key to this exercise is to live the experience as fully as you can. You are not passively watching a scene. You are creating as real an experience as you can for yourself.

In your imagination, see the place where you would be in order for your dream to be a reality. What sounds would be there? What people? What would they be saying to you or you to them? See if you can feel the textures that you would feel as well as the emotions that the scene would evoke if it were, in fact, really happening. If this proves too difficult at the beginning, try imagining a friend telling you how happy he is at seeing your dream fulfilled.

When you have finished your created scene, at this level of emotional reality, go to sleep for a few moments. The sleep will tend to seal the experience for you, making it as real as if it had actually happened.

The scene that you create for this exercise should always be one that implies the fulfillment of your goal. One of the benefits of the exercise is that, by practicing the technique at the level of emotional reality, you begin to alter your attitude. You begin to come from the position of *being* as opposed to that of *striving*. This will greatly affect your perception of your world and your abilities which, in turn, will put you on a new level of acceptance, making you more aware of opportunities available to fulfill your dream in the real world.

Here then is the formula:

1. A physical and mental state of quietness.

2. The bringing together, in your imagination, of everything that you will need.

3. The creation of a scene that implies the fulfillment of your dream or goal.

4. The living through of that scene at the level of emotional reality and feeling.

5. The deep relaxation into that feeling of accomplishment that fulfillment of your dream would bring.

6. The brief period of sleep to seal the experience.

By the way, this in no way differs from what you do every day of your life to create your present life situations. Remember, no goal comes to fruition without first taking shape as a plan. The difference is that the imagining you now do is haphazard and often negative. Use of the technique described here will enable you to consciously experience new levels of awareness.

If you feel like repeating the exercise with the same goal in mind, you may do this, but it really is not necessary. You should, of course, repeat it until you know that you have established the proper feeling. Once you have gone deep into the imagined feeling, you will have a comfortable feeling of fulfillment and you will know that you are ready to move on.

You will realize that you are coming from a position of *having* and *being* rather than that of *striving* when you find yourself acting, feeling and thinking in your daily life as though what you had imagined were in fact a reality.

This is not mumbo jumbo. If you were actually in the state of feeling that your dream implies, you would be doing the things that the feeling implied, and thus your dream would be embodied. The key is that you must be able to truly accept and believe in it. What that does, of course, is very safely keep you from wanting to walk on water or become sole ruler of the universe. You must be able to take responsibility for what you desire in order for this technique to work. You must be able to positively answer the question: If my dream were now a reality, could I accept it?

The result of most of our actions is dependent upon what we expect to happen. Therefore, we must learn to expect what we want. This has nothing to do with a nebulous "hope."

Rather it is a conscious plugging in to the dynamic "as if."

By allowing your imagination to focus on a desired result, you are preventing it from becoming overwhelmed by all the considerations with which people habitually weigh themselves down—all the catastrophic contingencies that we fear, that keep us immobilized and that therefore prevent us from realizing our goals. Using the technique described, you experience vividly what you desire as though it were true. This, in turn, acts as a practice session for your actions in the real world. You simply imagine what it would be like if it were impossible for you to fail, and you act as if that were so.

Do not project yourself into the future to experience your dream. Experience it vividly as though it were true now. You will know that you have done this successfully when you begin to act as though it were indeed true.

The use of creative imagination is not to be confused with auto-suggestion. When you consciously and vividly create how it would be for you if what you desire were true, you are awakening an inner knowingness in yourself to the point of seeing opportunities and possibilities as present realities. This is quite different from conditioning the subconscious mind.

By using your imagination in this way, you will be setting powerful forces into motion. Do everything you can not to interfere with their proper working. For example, try to avoid negative or doubting thoughts, and direct your conversation to the positive as well. This is not a casual suggestion that you turn into some kind of Pollyanna. It is merely a recognition of the fact that when you concentrate on negative images, you begin a negative cycle, and that the reverse is just as true. You can test this from your own experience. The next time you feel "down" and someone asks you how you are, instead of automatically repeating the litany of your woes, see if you can direct your thoughts and words to a more positive direction. If you can do this, you will find that you feel better at the end of the conversation.

Incidentally, I am not suggesting that you deny your feelings. Very often it is necessary to get in touch with the pain that we are feeling in order to accept it and move on. However, there is quite a difference between experiencing real pain and complaining about things. It is the latter that is to be avoided.

When you are unsettled and unsure, then this uneasiness is reflected in your real world. It is easy to believe that if only you could settle your affairs, then you would feel more at ease. Actually, the reverse is true.

As Ezra Pound said: A slave is one who waits for someone else to come and free him. If you are looking for change to take place in your life, you must first change your concept of your own limitations. When you can act upon your ideas with feeling, you will see your goals fulfilled at the level of reality.

By utilizing the technique of creative imagination you will be initiating a process of dwelling on a solution instead of a problem. This will free you to do the things that need to be done. And, obviously, if you do the things you need to do in order to transform your dream into a reality, then you cannot fail.

However, to repeat what I said at the start of this chapter, it doesn't really matter whether you believe in the technique or not. If you use it, you will be encouraging the development of your powers of visualization and thus improving your intelligence.

The Smallest
Chunks of Time

As we have discussed before, the key to mind expansion usually lies in opening the door to new ways of looking at things, in breaking down our habitual ways of perceiving. We have also discussed the possibility of liberating all "waiting time" and turning it into time available for creative use.

This chapter will detail exercises that you can use in the moments in-between, those tiny chunks of time that we usually dismiss as too short to use constructively. Some of these exercises literally take seconds, others take only a few moments. All serve to increase intelligence by expanding awareness.

Although I call them exercises, they should not be regarded as "assignments" or "chores." They are all stimulating if approached with an open mind, and they should be enjoyable.

By the way, though far from complicated, these are not moments that can be rushed through. Even though the exercises take only tiny amounts of time, they cannot be pushed. Take them moment by moment and do them thoroughly. Their power is reached through a gentle approach. I would also suggest some consistency. That is, you cannot expect to continue seeing and thinking on expanded levels unless you consciously maintain these levels.

My suggestion would be that you read each exercise through a couple of times. Try a few of them until you become familiar with them. Then pick two or three and use them repeatedly for a time. When? Whenever you have a few moments, or even a few free seconds.

1. *Looking and Seeing:* Choose any small object. It could be a rock, a pencil, a leaf, a coin—anything. Choose something that you have looked at many times, a common everyday object.

Now, hold the object in front of you and focus clearly on it. There is nothing to think about or analyze or figure out about it. Just take it in visually, concentrating on it. Notice every imperfection, every scratch. See what it is about this particular object that differentiates it from all other similar objects, and from everything else in the world.

As you focus in, the natural tendency will be to be pulled away by other things in your visual field. As you find yourself being distracted, return to the object. See if you can drop everything except the visual from this experience.

If you practice this exercise a few times, you will discover that you are seeing shapes and colors and curves that you have never seen before. Your ability to focus, to concentrate will be sharpened. And you will begin to know the difference between looking and seeing.

As you practice, be sure to contain this exercise into an alloted sixty seconds or so. That is long enough at the beginning. Otherwise, it will be too difficult to maintain full concentration, which is a requirement for this exercise as well as the ones that follow. So take a minute to really see something, then break away, go back to what you were doing before. And when you have another minute with nothing to do, pick another object, and really see it.

2. *Hearing and Listening:* Again you have sixty seconds. Close your eyes, stop all bodily motion and listen. There is nothing but sound in your world. Don't think about it, don't try to figure it out or to identify individual sounds. Just listen. Remain absolutely quiet. After sixty seconds, break away, go about your business. When you have another chance, take a minute and really listen.

3. *Tasting:* Choose a time when you are slightly hungry. Take a small bite of food, close your eyes, and slowly chew as you become aware of texture and taste. Don't think

about it. Exclude everything but the experience of taste.

These exercises may seem obvious and simple to you as you read them. Your experience of them, however, will reveal their gentle power. They are really quite subtle and can be complex as well as difficult. But if you do them consistently, you will find an increase in sensory awareness that is very rewarding.

4. *Touch:* This is similar to the previous exercises. Choose a small object and experience it only through touch. That is, do not look at it. Close your eyes and explore the object with your hands. Feel its texture, feel its weight. Don't think about it. Resist the temptation to put anything into words. Just feel it. Now place it against your cheek, roll it between your fingers. Do anything you can to know that object purely through your sense of touch. Again, only do this for sixty seconds of complete concentration. Then break for a while. Then, again, pick up an object and experience it through touch.

As you read through these exercises, you will probably recognize similarities between them and some that we discussed in the chapter on meditation. Once again, we are in the process of learning to expand by learning to focus and concentrate. It can be amazing what happens as you begin to experience control over habitual functions. You must be aware to be in control—and as you experience more control, you increase your awareness.

5. *Breathing:* Another exercise similar to meditation. Take sixty seconds. Very slowly, inhale. Now hold your breath for a count of four. Finally, exhale very slowly through your nostrils.

As you practice this exercise, begin to build up the time that you hold the breath. But be sure that you never hold it so long that you have to quickly expel the air. The object is to control the exhalation, to be in complete control of the breathing process. The exercise should be done slowly, rhythmically.

6. *Shifting Your Perspective:* We tend to conceptualize growth as something that happens in a linear fashion. That is, we imagine that we learn by moving forward. What is equally true, however, is that we can expand consciousness by moving in other directions. We have seen that this is true as we ex-

plored movement in an inner direction. Now, we will see that we can grow just by subtly shifting our perspective.

Choose a simple object and take it in visually. Now, use your imagination and see how it would look from the other side, without turning it around. Now visualize it as though seeing it from above, from underneath. Lastly, close your eyes and imagine you are inside it. What does it look like? What does it feel like? Is it cold in there? Warm? Bright? What? Take two or three minutes with this and slowly explore what the different vantage points do to your understanding of the object you have chosen.

7. *Finding Your Center:* By "center," I do not mean the center of your body. What I am referring to is that place within yourself that you experience as *you.* This is a very subtle exercise and should not be attempted until you feel comfortable with the preceding exercises. Notice that I said subtle, not serious. Approach this with ease. Yes, you will need full concentration, but of a gentle, not a forced sort. Take two or three minutes. Relax, close your eyes. Quiet the body. Focus within and see if you can locate where you are in your body. Feel that. Experience it. Don't look for something rational or explainable. Don't attempt to put it into words. Just find that place that is you. Be there with it for a moment. Then stop and return to what you were doing.

When you are quite comfortable with this, begin to add another step: Once you have zeroed in on your center—that place where you are in your body—imagine that that center is expanding, flowing slowly from its focal point throughout your body. Feel it as a warm expansion filling up your entire body.

8. *Seeing People:* This can be done any time, wherever and whenever you are in a situation where you are facing someone who is not aware of you. A public bus, or a waiting room— anywhere. Relax and look at the other person, trying to really see him or her. Focus your complete attention. Slowly look at each part of the person's face. Become aware of all the details that make that person unique. When you feel that you have really seen that person, relax and close your eyes. Slowly, comfortably, create that person in your imagination.

Another aspect of this exercise is to take a small chunk of

time to see yourself. You do this by closing your eyes, relaxing completely, and seeing a picture of your own face. See how you look to you. Many people have difficulty with this at first. Take your time and see if you can focus in on your own sense of how you look. Relax.

By the way, you may find it helpful to make brief notes on some of these experiences. Nothing extensive and nothing that interrupts your experience. But after doing one of the exercises, make a note of how you felt or anything that had a special meaning for you. As the days and weeks pass, you may find it helpful to look over your notes periodically. Sometimes it is difficult to keep track of changes that are subtle, and I think that you will be pleased, as you read your notes on your experiences, to follow the gradual expansion of your awareness.

9. *Feelings:* How do you look when you are angry? When you are afraid? When you are happy? Sad? In love? One way to find out is to take a few moments in front of a mirror. Close your eyes and concentrate completely on something that will arouse one particular emotion. Keep your eyes closed and let yourself be filled with that emotion. Let the feeling build. Now, open your eyes and look at your face. See the expression, the color, the lines formed. How does your mouth look? What about your eyes? Relax. Close your eyes. Choose another emotion and repeat the exercise. Notice the difference in the way that this emotion affects you.

10. *Expanding Your World:* This exercise is especially good to counteract those moments when something discouraging has happened, times when most people tend to shrink into themselves.

Find a place where you won't be disturbed for a few moments, close your eyes and relax. Now, locate your center. Take a moment. Experience where you are in your body. Now, imagine that your center is expanding—slowly growing until it fills up your entire body. Go slowly. There is nothing to figure out and you don't have to finish anything. Just let your center flow easily throughout your body until you can feel it filling you up.

Next imagine that your center is expanding, filling up the area around your body like a protective shield. A strong, safe border surrounding your body. Feel it there. Experience it. Now, imagine that it is expanding still further, until it has filled up the entire room. Take your time. Let it grow.

You can take this as far as you want to. You can expand as much as you want to. Your center can continue to grow until it encompasses the building you are in . . . the city . . . the nation . . . the planet . . . and on and on. Move slowly and naturally and experience the feeling that comes.

When you have completed this part of the exercise, slowly return step by step until you have brought yourself back into the room and back into your body. Take a moment. Open your eyes. Relax.

11. *Reliving An Emotion:* This exercise will take somewhat longer than the preceding ones. It has been placed after them only partially because of its length, however. It is fundamentally more complex than anything that has come before in this chapter and should be approached after you are quite comfortable with the preceding exercises.

Find a quiet, comfortable place where you won't be disturbed for the ten or twenty minutes that you will need. Close your eyes. Relax and find your center. Now, think of a time when you felt a strong emotion. It doesn't matter what emotional state you choose, just as long as you choose a specific incident that is very clear for you. Take your time and re-create that incident for yourself. Where were you? Visualize all the details of the place. See it as clearly as you can. Recall as many details as you can. Visualize yourself in that setting. Was someone else there? See that person as completely as you can. What was he or she doing? Saying? What were you doing? Make the situation as real for yourself as possible.

As you relive the experience, you may begin to feel bodily sensations. Where? In your throat? In your gut? You are feeling what you felt then? Feel it. Experience it. Recapture it. How did you feel during the experience? Light? Heavy? Active? Passive? Don't try to analyze what is happening. Just let yourself feel as strongly as you can. Let the emotion fill you entirely.

Slowly, let the feeling go. Relax. Let it gradually diminish. Come back to this moment. Relax. Open your eyes.

This can be a powerful exercise and should not be repeated

immediately. Allow at least a few hours between this and any other exercise. Simply go back to other things. Don't think about the experience. Don't try to figure it out.

If you have practiced the preceding exercises with any consistency, you will have discovered by now how full and rewarding your moments in between can be. Let these exercises become a part of your life. Call upon them often to enrich it. The exercises themselves, as you have seen, bring their own rewards. In addition, they lead to a gradual growth of awareness of self, of others and of the world around you. As your powers of perception develop, you will feel the quality of your experiences change.

Chapter 12

Special Techniques

The exercises in this chapter once again call on your imagination in challenging ways—with this difference, however: They are geared toward very specific results. That is, in the previous chapter, you learned techniques that would subtly alter your perceptions. In this chapter, you will learn techniques that you can use toward very specific ends.

Let me emphasize, as I have before, that you do not have to believe in these techniques. They work; but even if they didn't, the doing of the exercises has a consciousness-expanding effect.

1. *A Safe Space:* Find a comfortable position, close your eyes, and relax completely. Your arms and legs should be uncrossed and not touching. Mentally go over your body, and wherever you notice tension, simply bring your awareness there. Notice if it changes as you do so. Relax. Breathe easily and deeply for a few moments. Just let go. Now, begin to create a place in your imagination that can be your own private retreat. It could be a room in a building or it could be an enclosed area in the woods. Anyplace at all which represents a completely safe environment for you, a place where you can be totally at ease.

Make the scene as real as possible for yourself. Visualize as many details as possible. Exactly where are you? See the place as clearly as you can. Furnish your room in detail. The more exact you can be, the more reality the space will have for you, and the more use it can be to you later on.

Keep your eyes closed while you use your hands and create the walls yourself. Do you choose wallpaper or paint? What color? What texture? Build the furniture. Feel the different textures of each piece. What are the pieces that you need to have in order for this place to be perfect? Use everything that you have learned previously to create this very special space just as you want it. Be sure that, in addition to whatever regular doors and windows you might want, you also create a door somewhere that opens in such a fashion that it slides upwards from the bottom to open. This is important.

When you have completed your space, keep your eyes closed and—in your imagination—take a look around. Enjoy a few moments there. Experience yourself there and tell yourself that you will be able to return any time that you want to. Then re-create the room that you are in—still with your eyes closed—and when you have done that, open your eyes. Relax. Do something else for a while.

2. *Counselors:* Close your eyes, relax completely—and enter your space. Breathe deeply and imagine that a man and a woman are going to come into your space. Don't try to figure anything out. Don't try to put anyone there. Just allow for the possibility that first a man and then a woman will be standing behind your special sliding door. They will be coming to be of assistance to you, and you do not have to do anything at all about it. There is nothing to figure out, nothing to explain.

Now, imagine that a man is standing behind the special sliding door. You don't know who it is yet. Keep your eyes closed and breathe deeply. Relax. Very gradually, imagine that the door is sliding upwards so that you can now see the man's feet. Little by little, as the door moves upward, you can see more and more of the man in front of you. Keep your eyes closed and create the man with your hands. You still cannot see his face. Mold him with your hands and make him real for you. When you have completely created the rest of his body, allow the door to open completely so that the man is standing there in front of you. He may be someone that you know personally, or he may not be. He may be someone who died long ago—or he may be someone from the future. He may be someone who is famous or he may come from another world. See him there. Create him there. When he is completely there, welcome him into your space and talk to him for a few moments. Is there a question that you need answered? See what he says.

The sliding door, which closed as the man entered your space, now has a woman standing behind it. Go through exactly the same procedure with the woman as you did with the man. Do not rush. Take your time, and take what you get. You may be surprised by who arrives. You may be pleased. You may not be. It doesn't matter. Just relax and see what happens. Experience it as fully as you can.

The man and the woman are your counselors. They will be available to you at any time. They can answer questions for you and enable you to reach deeper levels of awareness. You have created a way for yourself to tap into another level of yourself for answers to problems or for any other use as you see fit. Do not try to figure this out. It has nothing to do with logic and everything to do with experience. Simply allow this to be so for you.

After you have talked with your counselors for a few moments, take your leave of them for now. Keep your eyes closed as you leave your space and re-create the room for yourself. When you have done this, open your eyes.

3. *The Witness:* Review this exercise in the chapter on meditation. Remember that the witness simply observes. The witness does not add evaluations or judgments. He simply notes what is going on at a particular moment.

4. *Specific Pain:* This is a technique to try on that headache or backache that won't go away. Close your eyes, uncross your arms and legs and relax completely. Enter your space. Take a few moments as you breathe deeply. Relax. Now, take a look at your pain. Do not try to change it or resist it in any way. Simply look at it and begin to articulate what you see and feel. What color is the pain? Where is it located—exactly? Do not settle for an approximation. Place the pain as located exactly so many inches in this direction and so many inches from there and so on. Does it seem to move? Is it a sharp pain or is it dull? Does it throb? How big is it? If it were liquid, how big a container would you need? Can you pour it into a container? Do that.

What does your pain make you think of? Does it remind you

of anything? Any place? Look at whatever comes up for you. Now return to its color. Has it changed? What about its shape and location? Is it the same as when you started? Keep your eyes closed and continue to look at this pain. Continue to be as specific as you possibly can. Add more and more details. How do you feel about it? Describe your feelings about it exactly. How does it make you feel? Relax. Breathe evenly. When you have continued with this as long as you want to (and at least for five to ten minutes), relax . . . re-create the room for yourself, and open your eyes.

You must experience this exercise and not try to figure it out. You may find that your pain totally disappears or it may diminish to a significant degree or you may have to repeat this process several times before you notice that the pain lessens. Simply do the exercise and see what happens.

5. *The Mirror:* This is a technique to use for problem solving. Close your eyes, relax completely and enter your space. Create and project in front of you a full length mirror. Imagine that the frame of the mirror can be mentally changed at will from black to white. When you use this mirror in the future, you will project a problem onto the mirror with the black frame. When you are creating the solution, you will always visualize it with the white frame.

To solve a problem with your mirror, you enter your space and then create an image of the problem (thing, person, or scene). You project this onto your black framed mirror and make a careful study of it. See it from all angles; look at it carefully. Do not try to change it. Just describe everything you can about the problem.

After you have studied the problem, erase the problem image, change the frame of the mirror to white, and create and project a solution image onto the white framed mirror. See this as clearly as you can. From now on, any time that you happen to think of the project, see it always in its solution form. Visualize it as the solution framed in white. As in the technique that makes use of the creative imagination, you never focus on the problem once you have made a careful study of it. You always visualize the solution.

6. *Deeper Levels:* Close your eyes, relax completely, enter your space. Breathe deeply and evenly for a few moments.

Now slowly bring together the tips of the first three fingers of each hand. Let yourself be totally quiet, completely relaxed. After a few moments, re-create the room and open your eyes. You will find that bringing the tips of the first three fingers of each hand together while in your space enables you to enter deeper levels of awareness. You may use this technique during any of the exercises described either in this chapter or in the chapter on meditation.

7. *Sleep:* Try this method instead of tossing and turning. Lie still in bed. That is, find a comfortable position and consciously quiet the body. Mentally go over your body and bring your attention to any area where you notice tension. Relax and breathe deeply. Have your eyes closed and enter your space.

Now, visualize a blackboard in front of you. Mentally take a piece of chalk and draw a large circle with it. Next draw an "X" in the circle. Carefully erase the "X" from within the circle starting at the center. Be careful not to erase the circle. Relax and breathe deeply. Now write a large number 100 in the circle. Mentally erase the number 100 from within the circle starting at the center. Be careful not to erase the circle. Relax. You are moving in the direction of sleep. There is no rush and there is nothing to figure out. Continue in this same manner with the numbers 99, 98, 97 and so on. Be steady and methodical. Between each number and the next, instruct yourself to relax. You are moving towards a more relaxed state, in the direction of sleep. Whenever you use this method, you will awaken refreshed and rested.

8. *Remembering Dreams:* This process has to be done in three separate steps. Do not go on to steps two and three until step one has started to work for you. Then remain at step two until that takes effect before you attempt step three. Do not set any arbitrary amount of time that you imagine it should take you to reach step three. If you go at your own pace, eventually you will be able to recall and understand your dreams. However, there is no rush to reach this goal: Simply by doing the exercise, you will be training your mind and deepening your awareness.

Step one: Close your eyes and enter your space. Relax. Now, mentally tell yourself that you want to remember a dream and that you are going to remember a dream. Have a paper and pencil nearby so that when you awaken—either during the night or in the morning—you will be able to write your dream down. Do not depend on memory for this. When you awaken with a vivid recollection of a dream, write it down immediately.

Once you have instructed yourself to remember a dream, go to sleep from this relaxed state. When you are satisfied that step one is working for you, go on to step two. Remember, that this might happen immediately, or it might take some time.

Step two: Close your eyes, relax and enter your space. Mentally tell yourself that you want to remember your dreams and that you are going to remember your dreams. Go to sleep from this relaxed state.

You may awaken several times during the night and in the morning with vivid recollections of dreams. Have paper and pencil ready to write them down. When you are satisfied that step two is working for you, go on to step three.

Do not be concerned if it takes a while for you to begin to remember your dreams. Just continue instructing yourself in a relaxed state and you will begin to be able to remember them.

Step three: When you reach this step, you can use this technique to generate a dream that you can remember, understand, and use for problem-solving.

Relax, close your eyes, and enter your space. Mentally tell yourself that you want to have a dream that will contain information to solve the problem that you have in mind. State the problem as specifically as you can and then add: "I will have such a dream, remember it and understand it." Go to sleep from this level of relaxation.

When you awaken with a vivid recollection of the desired dream, write it down. Again, it may take some time until you are proficient at this or it may come easily to you. Do not be concerned. With practice, you will be able to generate dreams, remember them and understand them.

9. *Awake:* Use this technique to awaken naturally, without an alarm clock. Relax, close your eyes and enter your space. Now, visualize a clock. Mentally move the hands of the clock

to indicate the time when you want to awaken and tell yourself mentally that you want to awaken at such and such time and that you will awaken at that time. Tell yourself also that when you awaken at your desired time you will feel wide awake, rested and refreshed. Go to sleep from this level of relaxation.

You may also use a similar technique to this when you find that you are sleepy at some time when you need to stay awake for some reason—for example, when you are driving or when you have some work that you must do, etc. Simply take a moment to imagine that you are in your space. It is helpful, of course, to take a few moments alone and to close your eyes while you do this, but if you have to, you will find that you can even do this in the presence of other people with your eyes open.

With this technique, you simply enter your space and notice what is going on with you—in this case, that you are sleepy. Notice that you are sleepy and tell yourself that when you come out of your space you will feel refreshed and awake. In effect, what you will be doing is acknowledging what is going on with you instead of fighting it and denying it. Once you have acknowledged it, you will find that you are able to move on.

Take your time with these techniques. Have some fun with them. And remember that every time that you practice any one of them, you will be flexing your mental muscles, building your control over previously automatic responses, and thereby increasing your awareness and your intelligence.

———◄◆►———

Chapter 13

What's Really
Going On?

Have you ever realized that something you thought was upsetting you was not really the basis of your upset? Have you
ever experienced a time when you knew that your upsets with
someone were of a more fundamental nature than any individual disagreement?

Maybe you have had these experiences, maybe not. But you
might consider the possibility that when we are upset in present time, it is because present circumstances remind us—on
a subconscious level—of past circumstances, and that they key
us into past responses, responses which may or may not be
appropriate.

All of us have past experiences which were traumatic to us
and which continue to influence the way in which we respond
to the world in the present. These parts of the past that we
carry around with us are images which we have of events and
people and places. Even if they were accurate images—and
because they are subjective, they cannot be—they would still
be images, imitations of the past filtered through a time warp.
The more concerned we are with the past, the less involved
we can be with the present. And, as we have discussed before,
the process of self-actualization always takes place in present
time.

There are ways in which you can involve yourself in a memory in order to find out what hidden power it holds over you

and what need is served by hanging onto it. By fully experiencing your memory you can learn to let go of it.

This chapter will demonstrate some ways in which you can investigate below the surface details of what you think is happening in a particular situation and relate them to what the situation really means to you on an emotional level. Once you come to understand what is really going on, you are free to deal effectively with it. As with other imagination exercises that we have discussed, the power of these processes resides in their experiential nature. They provide a cognitive expansion of intelligence.

(Incidentally, exercises like the ones that will be presented here and in other chapters have been used by fairly orthodox therapies, such as Gestalt, as well as the newer consciousness-expanding movements such as *est,* Silva Mind Control and Scientology. The fact that some of these movements contain elements that one might reject does not take away from the fact that some of the techniques that they use work. The ideas and techniques taken from these sources should be judged on their own merits.)

First, let us be certain that we understand what is meant by the term "upset." The dictionary defines it as a disorganization of behavior that occurs when an animal is under an environmental demand to which it is unready to respond.[1]

In other words, something happens that renders the animal helpless; that is, it is aware of some situation which it feels it must respond to, and for some reason it cannot respond appropriately, so it gets upset.

Werner Erhard defines "upset" in this way:

> To disturb the functioning, fulfillment, or completion of
> To disturb mentally or emotionally, or physically make sick
> To overturn or overthrow, especially unexpectedly
>   An upset is composed of the following three elements:
> Thwarted intention
> Unfulfilled expectation
> Undelivered communication

Reread the definition above so that you are sure that you clearly understand it. In terms of this definition, it is only possible to be upset about something when you intended or expected something else.

Now, take a pad and pencil and make a list of those things or people or events which continually seem to be the source of problems and upsets for you. The more specific you can be, the more value you will get from the exercise. Thinking about this is not sufficient; take the time to list as many upsetting things as you can. And don't worry: Although it may seem to you that you have hundreds of such items, you will discover by writing them down that you have, in fact, a finite number.

Set up your list in the following manner: In one column, list who or what the upset is with; in the second column, list where the upset takes place. In the next column list when it occurs. In the final column, list exactly what happens. See if you can leave all judgments and evaluations out of this unless you carefully note them as judgments and evaluations. What you are aiming for is to find out exactly what happens during a particular upsetting situation. So, for example, you would list that you get upset with Harry (Who); you get upset with Harry in restaurants (Where) whenever you have to meet him for lunch (When). What happens is that Harry agrees to meet you at a certain time, and you arrive at that time; you take up a table for forty minutes while the waiters keep asking you if you'd like to order and you feel embarrassed and you begin to get angry and you end up drinking more than you intended and eating all the bread; then Harry arrives and seems oblivious to the fact that he's kept you waiting again and you don't say very much about it because after all he is a good client; and you get upset.

You might even get more detailed than that. The point is just to say "and then this happens and then that happens and then the other thing happens." This gives you a chance to look at what is upsetting you, to begin to distance yourself from it. You may see the incident a little clearer just by going this far with the exercise.

As you list your recurring upsets, you may find that a pattern emerges: Focus on it a moment. Do you get yourself into these situations? Is there something that you are not doing now that you could do in the future to avoid the problem?

Once you have your list of upsets, close your eyes, relax completely, and become aware of your body. Simply bring your attention to your body and notice any areas of tension. Breathe deeply. Now bring your attention to your breathing for a few minutes. Relax. Now pick one upset from your list that seems very real to you at the moment, and quietly review all the facts surrounding it. Who or what is the upset with? Where does it occur? When? And what happens. Remember, what you are doing is just enumerating everything that happens in as non-judgmental a way as you can. Be as specific as possible. Exactly what happens?

After you have looked at the upset in this way, ask yourself if this particular upset is the result of a thwarted intention or an unfulfilled expectation or an undelivered communication. Do not try to figure out an answer. Take whatever comes to you. When you have answered that question, ask yourself if that thwarted intention, unfulfilled expectation or undelivered communication was moving toward you or away from you. In other words, was someone else's intention thwarted or was yours? Was it someone else's expectation that was unfulfilled or yours? Did someone fail to deliver a communication to you, or did you not deliver a communication?

As you continue, breathe deeply, keep your eyes closed, and relax. There is nothing to figure out. You are just looking at an upset. If, as you proceed you find at any time that the upset disappears (i.e., you are no longer upset about whatever it is) or that you have a realization about it, then consider that the process is over for now, relax for a few moments with your eyes closed, and then open your eyes.

If you still have the upset, recall an earlier similar upset. It is important that you do not intellectualize at this point. Take whatever comes to you as being an earlier similar memory even though you may not see any relationship between what is upsetting you now and what you remember at that moment.

With this earlier upset, ask yourself who or what the upset was with. Then ask where it happened and when. Then go over in your mind exactly what happened. Keep your eyes closed and continue to breathe deeply. Remember to be as specific as you can. Fill in as many details as possible. What did the room look like? If someone else was there what did he or she say? Was there a certain smell? Every detail that you supply brings you that much closer to pinning down what is at the root of your upset. Be aware of bodily sensations that may occur. Is there tension anywhere? Just notice what is happening with you.

Now, in this earlier upset, was your upset caused mainly by a thwarted intention, an unfulfilled expectation or an undelivered communication? Take a look and see. Don't try to be logical. When you have the answer, ask yourself if the thwarted intention or unfulfilled expectation or undelivered communication was mainly coming in or going out from you.

At any point during this process, you may have an understanding or a realization or an insight. If you do, allow yourself to fully experience it, relax for a few moments, and open your eyes. Do not attempt to deal with more than one upset from your list at a time. If you have some new understanding of it, fine. Leave this process and do something else for a while.

If you still have this upset, then recall a previous similar upset. Once again, take whatever comes to you. This is very important. What comes to you may be the same incident that you just went over; if so, choose that. Or you may remember something that you thought happened later; choose that. Or you may think of something which seems totally unrelated; choose that. Go through the same procedure that has been outlined in this chapter. Take your time. This process cannot be rushed. If you still have the upset when you have completed looking at this earlier, similar incident, then recall still another earlier, similar upset. Once again take whatever comes to you.

If the upset still remains, keep your eyes closed, breathe deeply, relax—and ask yourself if you are willing to give up this upset. Forget about shoulds and oughts here. Simply look and answer truthfully, not logically. If you are not willing to give up this upset right now, then simply relax for a few moments, open your eyes and do something else.

If you are willing to give up this upset, then once again ask yourself to recall an earlier similar upset and repeat the entire procedure again.

If, at the end of this, the upset still remains and you have not had a realization about it, then ask yourself this question: "What is the string that is tying me to this upset?" You may get an answer to this question. Whether you do or not, see if you can just let go of the string that ties you to the upset. Then take a few moments to relax before you open your eyes.

You may have experienced an exciting or emotionally moving cognition during this process, or you may not have. Do not be concerned. As you continue to practice, you will become more comfortable with this exercise, and you will be able to get more and more out of it.

Even if you are still upset about whatever it was you looked at during this particular session, it is almost impossible that you feel the same way about it as you did before. The process provides an invaluable way of looking into your own experience to find out what is really true for you.

When something from the past continues to influence us in the present, it is usually because there is something unfinished about it. By investing yourself in this unfinished situation on an experiential level, you can become aware of feelings and actions that were unexpressed or incompleted, and let them come to rest. Here is another exercise that will enable you to experience working with this kind of unfinished situation.

Get into a comfortable position, close your eyes, and relax completely. Keep your eyes closed throughout the exercise. Go over your body and simply notice any points of tension, any discomfort. Simply let your attention be on your body, and what is going on with you right now. As you do this, you may notice that certain bodily sensations change. Just notice. Be aware. Now bring your attention to your breathing. Don't manipulate your breathing at all. Simply be aware of it. As you become aware of it, does it change? Simply notice.

Next bring your attention to your feelings. How are you feeling right now? And again—right now? Now, let go of your feelings. This does not mean "do not have feelings." It just means that your attention is no longer focused on how you are feeling at the moment.

Take a deep breath—slowly—and then slowly release the breath. Once again, breathe deeply and then slowly release. Do this three or four times.

Now breathe naturally, watching as your breath goes in and out evenly, and imagine that each breath removes any remaining tension from your body.

Now, recall a time when you wanted to say "No," but you actually found yourself saying "Yes." Just relax and take a look and put yourself back into that situation as though it were happening right now. See if you can create the scene in front of you. Try to visualize it, filling in as many details as you possibly can. Make it real for you. What is the place like? Who else is there? What are you saying? What is the other person saying? See how fully you can invest yourself in this experience. See if you can experience it and relive it as if it were happening right now.

At the moment when you say "Yes," do you feel good about it? Bad? How do you feel? Do you gain something by saying "Yes?" Do you avoid something? Take a look at what it means to you to say "Yes" in this situation.

Now, in your imagination, go back and re-create the scene up to the moment before you said "Yes." This time allow yourself to say "No," and also complete the communication. What was left unsaid before? Say it now. How does all this make you feel? Is the other person responding? How? How does that make you feel? And what do you say?

All right. Keep your eyes closed. Relax. Right now, see if you can change places and become the person to whom you were talking. Can you create this experience from that person's point of view? How do you feel and what do you say? Do you like how you are as this person? Do you feel stronger as yourself or as the other person? See if you can speak directly to this person and tell him exactly how you feel.

Continue this process by becoming yourself again and then the other person. See how fully you can experience being this other person. How do things look to him? What is it like from his point of view? How is it, exactly, from your point of view? What is the difference between you? See if you can put this into words. How do you feel now about the exchange? Are you fighting and arguing or does there seem to be more genuine communication now? Is there anything that you haven't said? See if you can say that.

Have your feelings about the other person changed? How?

Tell him how you feel about him. Relax. Don't force in any way. Leave out all the preambles and the excuses and the clauses leading up, and simply tell the other person what you need to tell him. How does that make you feel?

Now become the other person and do the same thing; that is, how does the other person react to what you've said? How do you feel about that?

Remember that this is not an intellectual exercise. Allow yourself to fully experience exactly what things are like for each of you. Experience being these two people as though you were having this experience *right now*. Explore how you interact with each other.

Now take a few moments just to absorb the experience. Breathe deeply. Relax. Open your eyes.

Usually, in a situation in which there is conflict, we identify mostly with one side, and we don't see our contribution to the opposing side. As we identify with both sides, we can become more balanced and centered. By re-experiencing some past event in the present, we can discover what we left unfinished or unexpressed. This enables us to complete the experience. Remember that this process is something that must be lived through. It cannot be forced or manipulated in any way. It must be allowed to happen.

The fact that you choose an event, re-create it in the present and experience it does not guarantee that it will immediately cease to have power over you. You may have to return to the same event a few times to fully remove the charge it has. But each time that you do so, your feelings about it will change. You can return to it until it has been fully experienced and you can let it go.

This exercise will also enable you to look at what saying "Yes" does for you as well as what it does *to* you. Some people say "Yes" all the time. Some say "No" all the time. Very few people take the time to fully realize what goes on in them as they comply. It is only by allowing ourselves to be fully aware of what is going on within us at any time that we can work through the opposing forces within us and find out what we really want to do at any particular time. This puts us in touch with ourselves and puts the element of choice back into the situation. Through this process, we become able more and more to respond honestly and directly without needing the support, approval or permission of others.

To the extent that you are still concerned about events from the past, you are not fully experiencing what is going on here-and-now in the present moment. The more that you deal with people based on your past experience of them or of other people, the less you can experience them just as they are now. The more colored your perceptions are by your regrets and resentments from the past, the less likely it will be that you can respond to events and people without your reactions being influenced by these warped perceptions. Until you can come to terms with these uncompleted communications and experiences and are able to express the feelings that you held back, you will continue to be influenced by them.

This is especially noticeable in relationships with people who are the most important to us. Often, even after such people are no longer a part of our lives (as when a parent dies, for example), we unconsciously still look to them for approval and support in some way. Most of us have residual feelings in regard to some people, and these unfinished situations interfere with and influence our present relationships. To the extent that you are living in the past, you cannot be living in the present. The next exercise can help you to clear up some of the unfinished memories you have with your parents.

Sit in a comfortable position, close your eyes and relax completely. Now, visualize your father sitting opposite you. Put him there. Create him there. See how real you can make this for yourself. What is he wearing? What is his expression? What is going on right now? Notice as many details as you can.

Now, see what things you can tell your father that you have always wanted to tell him but have previously held back. Talk to him exactly as though he really were right there in front of you. Tell him everything that you need to. Are there feelings of love that were previously unexpressed? Feelings of anger or disappointment or resentment? Tell him anything that you have been unable or unwilling to say before. How do you feel as you do this? What is going on in your body as you do this? Take your time. Say everything that you want and need to say to him.

Now, see if you can become your father. What is it like from his point of view? How do you feel about your child now? Answer yourself as your father, coming from his point of view. Be as direct and truthful as you possibly can. Re-create how things look from his point of view. How does that make you feel? Have your feelings changed in any way? Are you arguing with each other, or do you feel that there is real communication between you? Take a look and see.

Now switch places again. How do you respond to what your father just said? How do you feel? What do you say now? See if you can tell him exactly what you need from him and what you think of him. Tell him specifically what you wish he would do and be aware of how you feel as you do this. If it is difficult for you to speak to him, tell him this.

Now become your father again. As your father, how do you respond to what your child has just said? How do you feel? What understanding do you have of him? Can you identify with his feelings? Have you ever felt the same way? Now tell your child what you need and want from him.

Continue in this way, switching places and becoming first yourself and then your father. Notice if the quality of the dialogue changes. Does hostility grow or diminish between you? Does understanding grow or diminish? Identify as strongly as you can as yourself and as your father. When you are being yourself, see if you can discover what you gain by holding on to these unfinished feelings toward your father.

Now become your father and respond to this. What do you feel? What do you say? What is the relationship like now? Switch places again. How do you experience your relationship now? Do you have any different understanding of your father now? Tell him what is going on with you right now.

Relax completely. Now tell your father those things that you appreciate about him. No matter how much conflict there is in your relationship, there must be some things about him that you appreciate. Talk to him about these. Be specific.

Now become your father again and see how you respond to what your child just told you. Can you accept being appreciated in this way or do you minimize and reject what you've been told? Now, as your father, express your appreciation of your child. Tell your child in detail those things about him that you like and appreciate.

Now become yourself again. How do you respond to what your father just said? How do you feel about him now? Continue this dialogue, switching roles whenever you want to. Pay attention to the feelings that are aroused. Pay attention to whatever bodily sensations you have. Notice what is going on in the interaction and be as explicit as you can. For example, if your father is scolding you, then point this out and see if you can explain how that makes you feel. See how much you can express and clarify about this relationship.

It may take many sessions of such imaginings to clear up a relationship, but each time you go through this process you will have a deeper understanding of the dynamics involved in what happens between you. Go through the same process using your relationship with your mother or any significant other person in your life. It doesn't matter whether the person involved is living or dead. If there is something incomplete in the relationship, some words that need to be said or feelings that need to be expressed, allow yourself to experience these so that you can work them through and clarify whatever is bothering you.

Eventually, through using exercises such as the ones outlined above, you will learn to be able to let go of these past relationships, to give up your demands that these people be different, and to forgive them for what they are and what they aren't, and what they did or didn't do for or to you. You will begin to understand experientially that they couldn't be any other than as they are. As you begin more and more to clear up these past relationships, you can become more and more involved with the living people around you.

———◆▶——

Chapter 14

The Alive Body.

Throughout this book, we have examined methods of increasing intelligence by expanding knowledge—both logical and intuitive. But as Fritz Perls, among others, has noted, the organism always works as a whole: "We are not a summation of parts, but a *coordination*—a very subtle coordination of all these different bits that go into the making of the organism."[1] In our desire to grow intellectually, we must not forget the body.

It is not my purpose here to discuss physical exercises or muscle tone. What I am talking about is much more fundamental than that. It has to do with an inability to genuinely experience knowledge (as opposed to gathering information) unless we filter our experience through a body that is alive, vibrant.

The suggestions in this chapter are not physical exercises in the traditional sense. Their aim is to bring the body alive, and if they are done mechanically, they cannot achieve that result. The primary source for this chapter is Alexander Lowen, one of the founders of bioenergetic analysis.

Using the principles developed by Wilhelm Reich as a starting point, bioenergetic analysis works through the body to get to the emotions. Part of the therapy revolves around very specific physical work, often placing the body in stress positions. The particular and individual way in which one responds to the stress positions enables the therapist to diagnose how a particular person reacts to stress in life. It also often enables an individual to tap into traumas much more quickly than in conventional therapy. The body is worked with because it is postulated that traumas are lodged in the body as well as in the psyche. Sometimes the physical work can open up the breathing and the emotions in dramatic ways. Much of it is aimed at making the body feel grounded, literally able to stand on its own two feet.

The physical work is an integral part of the bioenergetic analyst's work; however, it is altogether possible to separate it out from the therapy, as it has a value in and of itself. Dr. Lowen recognizes this and, in fact, the Bioenergetic Institute in New York conducts weekly classes where the emphasis is totally on the physical work and no "therapy" takes place. In addition, patients are encouraged to do the physical work at home.

According to Lowen, a body that is "alive" is a source of pleasure and pride. When this is not the case, the person rejects his body. He may ignore it completely or he may undertake diets or weight-lifting programs or engage in a myriad of other activities in an effort to transform his body and make it more acceptable.

> However, as long as the body remains an object to the ego, it may fulfill the ego's pride, but it will never provide the joy and satisfaction that the "alive" body offers.
>
> The alive body is characterized by a life of its own. It has a motility independent of ego control which is manifested by the spontaneity of its gestures and the vivacity of its expression. It hums, it vibrates, it glows. It is charged with feeling. People are so accustomed to thinking of the body as an instrument or a tool of the mind that they accept its relative deadness as a normal state.
>
> They must [learn to] accept the relevance of their physical condition to their mental functioning. . . . They must experience their physical tension as a limitation of personality, and the release of this tension as a liberation of the personality. The discovery that the body has a life of its own and the capacity to heal itself is a revelation of hope.[2]

What follows is a discussion of some of the basic positions of stress and exercises that were developed by Lowen and his associates. (Anyone interested can find a more detailed presentation in Dr. Lowen's books, *Pleasure* or *The Betrayal of the Body*.) Once again, it must be emphasized that these positions cannot be done mechanically. If they are used to gain feeling in the body, they can be surprisingly effective despite their deceptive simplicity. There are no time limits: You simply maintain a position for as long as it produces meaningful sensations for you.

At first you will probably be able to maintain these positions only for brief periods of time. Start slowly and begin by holding a stress position for no longer than two minutes. The purpose of the exercises is to promote one's breathing, not to build endurance.

Almost invariably, people who do these special exercises experience tingling sensations in various parts of their bodies. You may also experience some dizziness. As your capacity to tolerate higher levels of oxygen increases, the dizziness will disappear. Sometimes you will experience sadness, longing and even crying. These emotions, in turn, may give way to anger. Simply allow yourself to experience whatever comes up for you as you make use of these positions. Go with your experience as fully as you can. At the same time, do not manipulate yourself because you expect to have certain sensations. Simply see what happens.

1. *Arching Backward:* This is the basic bioenergetic breathing exercise and is best done by arching backward over a rolled up blanket on a stool two feet high. (See the illustration.) If possible, the stool should be placed in such a way that the head and arms, which are extended backward, hang over or touch the bed which the stool is placed next to or alongside of. Keep the mouth open and allow the breathing to develop freely and easily. Most people tend to hold their breath in this position, as they do in most stress situations. You must consciously counter this tendency. Have the legs parallel, the feet flat on the floor about twelve inches apart. Bring your awareness to your pelvis and allow it to hang freely. The places where you notice pain while doing this exercise, such as in the lower back, will indicate to you areas of tension. If you can

begin to relax into the position, the breathing will become deeper and fuller and more abdominal. Be sure that the rolled-up blanket is placed between the shoulder blades at first. Eventually, you can vary the position to mobilize different muscles of the back.

At first you may feel that you are choking in this position. Do not be alarmed. Simply hold the position for a moment or two to begin with. The deep breathing that the position enduces can open the way for emotions to break through. Allow this to happen. Eventually, you will be able to use this position regularly to open your breathing and to relax tension that develops between your shoulders.

After maintaining this position for a minute or two, you reverse the position with another exercise.

2. *Bend Forward:* In this exercise you bend forward to touch the ground with your fingertips. (See the illustration.) The feet are about twelve inches apart, the toes turned slightly inward and the knees slightly bent. The hands are used only for balance. There should be no weight on them. Have the head hang down as loosely as possible. The weight of the body falls midway between the heel and ball of the foot. As you maintain this position, experiment with the amount of flexion in the knees. You will find different sensations emerge

as you place more or less stress upon the leg muscles. Have the breathing be abdominal. In this position, you should begin to feel your legs and feet vividly. As the feeling in the legs and feet increases, breathing automatically deepens. You may become aware of tension in the calf muscles and in the hamstrings. Begin to sense the quality of your contact with the ground. Is it secure? Spread your toes slightly and press down on your feet to increase contact with the ground.

Eventually a tremor of the legs will develop. This may or may not spread to other parts of the body. The vibration is due to the natural elasticity of the body and its normal reaction to stress. Vibration is a sign of life, and it is always experienced as pleasurable.

3. *The Bow:* Here is another stress position that can serve to deepen the breathing and increase awareness of the body. Stand with your feet about thirty inches apart with the toes turned inward. The knees should be bent as much as possible. Be sure that you are not holding yourself up but are letting your weight drop as much as possible into your legs. Now arch your back and place your hands on your hips. (See the illustration.) As you arch your back, be sure that your head

stays straight; that is, do not allow your head to drop back.
Your eyes should be level, your sight line directly in front
of you. In this position, the line of the body from the heels
to the back of the head forms an arc; the breathing should
be abdominal and relaxed. Do not be concerned if this
position is difficult to maintain. Simply assume the position
and become aware of your bodily sensations. You should
begin to sense increased perception of your legs. They may
begin to tremble. That is part of the design of the position.
You will begin to have an increased awareness of your ten-

sions through this position. That is also one of its functions.

As you come more in contact with specific areas of tension, you will begin to experience your areas of weakness. As your body becomes better integrated and coordinated, you will be able to maintain these positions for longer periods of time and with greater ease. And once the body becomes charged with life, you will experience it in a different way. In a very real sense, these positions will awaken your awareness of your ability to "stand on your own two feet," to feel grounded. Remember, they are not exercises, and if they are done mechanically, you will not experience the desired result.

The repetitive use of these positions has a cumulative effect. Each time that they are used, the breathing will become deeper and freer, which, in turn, will allow more sensations to arise in the body.

The following active movements are used to complement the passive positions just described in order to aid in developing awareness of feelings and ability to express them.

4. *Kicking:* This is one of the simplest and easiest expressive movements. Simply lie flat on a bed with your legs outstretched and kick up and down in a rhythmic and forceful manner. As you develop freedom in doing this, the wave of the movement will cause the head to whip up and down with each kick. This total bodily response is not possible if the body is held stiffly or if strong neck tensions prevent the head from moving. Experiment until you learn to give in to the movement. Although this is a very simple exercise, it will enable you to feel more alive, more energetic and more relaxed.

As you continue to practice, you will find that your early awkward and uncoordinated movements will become more integrated and that you will tire less easily.

5. *Hitting:* In this movement, you repeatedly strike a couch or a bed with either your fists or a tennis racquet. This serves both to release agression and to develop coordination and control. (See the illustration.)

These movements are expressive movements. To kick and to hit is to protest, and everybody has something to protest or kick about. Lack of coordination in either of these movements is a sign that you have not committed yourself fully to the activity. Your inability to do this should be looked at

carefully. Telling yourself that you "have no reason to be angry just now" should be recognized as just what it is: rationalization. A healthy person can identify with a feeling of anger sufficiently to permit him to execute the movements of hitting or kicking in a coordinated manner. Incoordination reflects inability to expreess feeling, and the physical procedures outlined will help you to improve in this area.

The mobilization of a body that is not accustomed to being charged is a slow process. Some discomfort or even pain may be experienced as contact is reestablished. There may also be periods of fatigue. This is to be expected and should not be resisted.

Here are some other activities that you can use to bring vibrancy back to the body.

6. Lie on a firm surface, face up. The legs should be bent, the feet about fifteen inches apart and flat against the surface you are on. Place your hands on your abdomen and bring your attention to your breathing, which should be abdominal. Simply breathe and be aware.

7. Take the same starting position except that your hands now are at your sides, palms down. Very slowly bring your knees towards each other until they almost touch. The feet maintain contact with the floor. Before the knees actually touch, slowly move them apart until they are beyond the starting position and in a slightly more open one. Then steadily and very slowly repeat these movements for a while, bringing the knees first towards each other and then away from each other. Even five minutes of this activity can prove enormously helpful. The rewards are completely out of proportion to the amount of energy expended in doing it. Simply allow yourself to experience the sensations that you begin to become aware of.

8. Lie on your back with your arms at your sides. The legs should be perpendicular to the floor and somewhat apart. The knees are slightly bent, the feet in extreme flexion. (See the illustration.) Maintain this position for a while, experimenting with the degree of flexion in the

knees. You might also try holding your toes with your hands.

The last suggestion for this chapter calls once more on your use of the creative imagination.

9. Sit in a comfortable position with your eyes closed. Imagine that at your very center there is a core of strength that is like a stream of water rising up through you. As you know, water in motion has flexibility. When directed in a stream—as from a water hose—it also has power. Get the feeling of this kind of strength within you.

When you experience the world around you, what you are really feeling is your body. For example, when your hand rests upon my arm, what I feel is the warmth in my arm that your hand produces. All feelings are body perceptions.

Self-awareness, too, is a function of feeling. Through awareness of the body, a person begins to know who he is. When he is aware of what is going on within his body, he comes in contact with himself. On the contrary, when a person is not in touch with his body from within, it feels strange and awkward, which makes him self-conscious in expression and movement. The person who doesn't feel his legs lacks a sense of security. The person who is unaware is also one whose image of himself does not coincide with the picture he presents to others.

Loss of self-awareness is caused by a chronic type of tension that is persistent, unconscious and that has become part of the body's structure or way of being. Relaxed muscles, on the contary, are muscles that are charged with energy. The positions, activities and exercises that I have described in this chapter are ways that you can use to locate that energy and make it available to you.

> Apart from the body, life is an illusion. In the body, one will encounter pain, sadness, anxiety, and terror, but these are at least real feelings, which can be experienced and expressed. The ability to feel pain is also the capacity to feel pleasure. To give in to tiredness is to find the peace of rest. Every bodily feeling implies its opposite. To be without feeling is to exist in a vacuum, cold and lifeless.[3]

Chapter 15

—◄◆►—

The Physical Brain

There is a simple fact whose consequences are usually ignored: It is that your brain is very much a physical part of that machine which is your body. If you think about this, you can verify from your own experience how your mental capacities seem diminished during periods of illness or lethargy and also how alert and sharp you feel mentally after certain kinds of exercises and experiences. And yet, usually—if you are like most people—you take your body (and therefore your brain) for granted.

My intention here is not to discuss the many physical exercises that are valuable for toning the body; what I will center my discussion on is aspects of the physical that relate especially to enhancing brain function. This is not to say that all physical exercises do not in some way affect your brain, but only that, with most, this is an incidental occurrence, while with others there is a more direct effect.

As with the rest of your body, the network of arteries and capillaries that supplies energy to the brain is a highly intricate and complex one. It is obvious that this circulatory system must be efficient or excessive cell damage and cell death will occur. Of course, you have billions of brain cells, and most of them are never used; they remain undeveloped. Still, the more loss you can prevent the better. And there are specific steps that you can take to prevent brain-cell damage and loss as well as to improve the circulatory system of the brain.

One very simple way to do this is to use the breath-holding

meditation exercise. Recent scientific research reveals that this ancient technique increases the carbon dioxide level of the bloodstream. It accomplishes this by opening the carotid valves so that more blood flows past. Although this increase in carbon dioxide level is momentary, its result is to improve the circulatory system sending oxygen to the blood. If you do this exercise often enough, the temporary carbon dioxide increase turns into something that happens often, and the valves then get into the habit of opening wider. In this way the entire circulatory system of the brain is built up.

There is currently a program used by Philadelphia's Institutes for the Achievement of Human Potential which is aimed at improving brain function and raising the intelligence; training of the carotid valves is one of the most important elements in the program. The researchers at the Institute have developed their own technique to accomplish this CO_2 training. It is called masking, and it is a simple method in which you re-breathe your own breath for a half a minute every half hour using a paper bag. Somehow the thought of putting a paper bag over my head makes me feel claustrophobic, so I prefer the meditation exercise, but certainly masking is a simple procedure and, if it appeals to you, is worth trying.

Please be sure, however, that you do choose a paper bag. The bag must be porous, and in any event, never do this exercise for longer than a half a minute at a time. It is also helpful if someone else is around if you try this technique. That is another reason why I prefer the meditation exercise. Although the masking technique is simple, it is also awkward and there is always this lurking discomfort about the possibility of cutting off necessary air supply. See how you feel about it, and decide if this exercise is for you.

Certain sports have a similar effect on the valves as the breath-holding exercise or masking. Jogging and underwater swimming are especially helpful. Of course, these are generally good exercises anyway. It should be noted, however, that the breath-holding exercise and the masking technique have been more effective than these when it comes to having a direct effect on the brain.

One form of overall exercise that is aimed at affecting the mind is Yoga. We have previously discussed two aspects of the practice of Yoga, the breathing and concentration exercises. Still another part of Yoga consists of physical postures or *asanas* which are aimed at increasing body flexibility, releasing tension, increasing energy and quieting the mind.

Variations of the Yogic postures have been absorbed into many kinds of more familiar forms of dance and exercise, and Hatha Yoga itself has become increasingly popular. (The term Hatha Yoga refers to that part of Yoga which includes the cleansing, stretching, and breathing techniques. The other major part of Yoga that we have considered is called Raja Yoga, and this is concerned with the mental techniques.)

The advantages inherent in the practice of Yoga are so many that it provides an ideal way in which to achieve its goals. For one thing, you need no expensive equipment or large area. All that is required is a private place and a mat or towel to sit on. Then, too, Yoga achieves results through very brief periods of practice. In addition, if your practice is fairly regular, you will begin to see results almost immediately.

Here are the principles for practicing the physical postures:

1. When you decide to approach the practice of Hatha Yoga, be as methodical and mechanical as possible. You cannot be haphazard about the practice of the Yoga postures. Although you will see some results no matter how brief your periods of practice, you must follow the instructions exactly to receive optimum benefits. This is mostly a matter of mindset, of approaching your practice with attention.

2. A simple rule of thumb is that if it hurts it isn't Yoga. Never tug, strain or pull. You cannot force your body into flexibility. Forcing actually slows down your progress, since it will cause your body to resist. Yoga is not competition, either with yourself or with anyone elese. Be gentle. Stretch until you reach the point beyond which it would hurt. As you continue practicing, your abilities will increase without effort on your part, simply by repeatedly doing the postures.

3. The movements of Yoga are designed to be carried out slowly. Quick movement through the postures does not achieve the same results. Slow motion is one of the keys to successful practice of the physical postures.

4. When you reach that point of your ultimate comfortable stretch, hold each posture motionless. Do not adjust your

body in any way during the few seconds that you maintain this position. Everything will happen automatically if you simply hold the posture as motionless as you possibly can in the final position.

5. Come out of each posture as slowly as you go into it. Never collapse or fall out of a posture. Never hold a posture so long that you must come out quickly. Keep the movements steady, slow and controlled at all times.

In this section, I will discuss some of the more accessible *asanas*. This is not to be interpreted in any way as a complete discussion of the available postures, but simply as an introduction to the subject or—for those of you already somewhat familiar with it—a possibility to review the postures in the context provided by this book. For each posture, read, understand and then experience.

The Alternate Leg Pull: Sit on the floor with your legs extended straight out in front of you. The knees should be straight, the toes and heels together. Let your hands rest on top of your thighs and your torso be as erect as possible. This is the beginning position for many of the forward bending postures.

Now, bring your left foot up until you can grasp it with both hands. Place the sole of your left foot against the inside of your right thigh. Your left heel should be as close to your groin as comfort permits. Remember, do not force.

Next raise both of your arms in front of you and bring them above your head, and then—in slow motion—twist slightly to the right so that you can move directly over your right leg. Now bend forward until you can grasp your right leg with your hands. Depending upon how flexible you are, you will be grasping either your thigh, your knee, your calf, your ankle or your foot. Do not be concerned about how far down you can go. With regular, methodical practice you will be able to reach farther down the leg until you attain full flexibility.

You have now reached the point where you have stretched to your maximum. This is the position that you will hold. Maintain this position, motionless, for a slow count of ten. Do not move in any way. The ultimate position—and your eventual aim—will be to have your forehead rest upon the knee of your extended leg.

Remember not to force your body in any way. You cannot be frivolous in your practice of Yoga, but at the same time your Yoga practice should be enjoyable. You should feel stretching sensations, but no feelings of pain or real discomfort if you are doing the postures correctly.

To come out of the posture, you reverse the movements that you took to enter it. Release your leg slowly and slowly raise up to your starting position. The bottom of your spine should straighten up first, then the middle of your back. The head comes up last.

Now straighten your left leg out in front of you and bring your right foot up against the inside of the left thigh. You are now ready to reverse the posture and to perform the exact same movements on the opposite side. Remember to move in a slow, relaxed and composed manner throughout.

After a period of time, you may want to increase the time that you hold the posture. Again, do this slowly. Do not attempt to hold the posture so long that you feel discomfort at any point in the practice of it.

The Cobra: Lie on your stomach with your hands at your sides, the face resting on one cheek. Relax completely. Now rest your forehead on the floor and—in slow motion—begin moving your head forward until it begins to leave the floor.

Allow your head to keep moving up using your neck muscles, until your neck cannot arch back any farther. Now begin to use your back muscles. Continue raising your head and torso up and back until you have reached your maximum.

Remember to keep your heels together throughout. This may seem more difficult at first, but as you continue your practice your spine will stretch in the correct way. When you keep the heels together, the pressure exerted by the posture is concentrated in a line down the center of the spine rather than being diffused throughout the back.

When you have reached the point beyond which you can no longer raise your trunk with the use of your back muscles alone, slowly bring your hands up to a position beneath your upper chest near your shoulders. The hands are in a position similar to that which they would assume in order to do a push-up. Now raise your torso up and back a little farther. Your hands and arms are to be used mainly for support and as little pressure as possible should be exerted on them.

When you have reached your maximum position, hold that position motionless for a slow count of ten. Breathe normally as you do this. Remember not to force in any way. If you simply go as far as you can and hold that position for several seconds, eventually the body will stretch by itself and you will be able to achieve the complete posture. Do not set any arbitrary schedule for this. Obtain the maximum stretch that you can for your body right now, and the rest will take care of itself.

For each posture, remember to begin by relaxing completely. Then enter the posture slowly, maintain the farthest point for several seconds, and come out of the posture as slowly as you entered it.

As you come out of the Cobra position, hold your head back as far as possible until the last moment. It may help to use your eyes throughout. If you keep them looking up throughout the posture, you will automatically hold your head back. When you reach the point at which you no longer need your arms to support your back as you are returning to the beginning position, bring your arms back to your sides and continue coming down until your chest rests on the floor. Then lower your head until finally your forehead is resting on the ground. Turn your face on your cheek and relax completely.

There are five parts to the practice of any of the *asanas*. We have discussed the need for total relaxation before entering a posture, the slow entering of the posture, the holding, and the slow return to the starting position. The last part is of equal importance to the other four, and it is simply this: In between the practice of one posture and the next, it is important to take some time simply to relax. This is not time to daydream or to move around. It is definitely part of your practice. You simply take a few seconds or a few moments to experience the benefits of the posture and to relax completely before going on to the next posture.

Back Stretch: Sit in the beginning position as described for the alternate leg pull. Slowly raise both your arms straight out in front of you; have the thumbs together and the backs of your hands at eye level.

Now, lean back a few inches. Keep your back as straight as

possible and your chest as far up and out as you can. This will stretch your rib cage and your waist and will make certain that you receive the greatest stretching effect as you move into the next part of the posture.

Now slowly come forward until you grasp the farthest part of your legs that comfort permits. Do not be concerned about how far you can reach. Let your elbows bend slightly and gently pull forward, aiming your head toward your knees. Keep moving forward until you have stretched just the right amount for you. Do not strain in any way. The stretching sensation should be mild and enjoyable. If it hurts, then you are going beyond your capabilities of the moment. Relax.

Once you have reached the point of your ultimate stretch, maintain that position without moving for a slow count of ten. Once again, this holding part of the exercise will be increased over a period of time. But begin by holding the posture for ten seconds only. Remember that you are not to move in any way during this holding time. Do not attempt to stretch farther. Simply breathe normally and relax and hold the posture.

To come out of the posture, simply reverse the steps that you took to enter it. Remember to move slowly and steadily. When you have returned to the starting position, lie back in *Savasana* for a few moments. (See the chapter on meditation for a review of what is meant by this posture.)

The Plough: Lie on your back with your legs together, your arms at your sides, palms down. Relax completely. Now tighten your abdominal muscles and raise your legs slowly so that they form a ninety-degree angle with the floor.

At this point, begin to use your hands. Apply pressure against the floor at your sides, and raise your buttocks and lower back off the floor so that your legs rise over your body with the feet moving over your head. The feet keep moving over the head, and if you breathe regularly and do not strain, gravity will slowly bring them to the point at which they will touch the floor behind you. Remember to move as slowly as possible. When your toes touch the floor behind your head, hold this position for a slow count of ten.

To come out of the plough, reverse your movements. Use your hands for support, and unroll your back slowly, vertebra by vertebra. This is as much a part of the posture as the holding position, and it is very important that you move very slowly. When your back is completely unrolled, your legs will once again be at a ninety-degree angle from the floor. From this position, slowly lower them to the floor. Then take the position of *Savasana* and relax for a few moments.

The Locust: Lie face down with your cheek to the side and relax completely. The arms are at the sides of your body, palms up. Now bring your heels and toes together, the toes extending outward, and place your chin on the mat. Clench your hands into fists so that your thumbs are pointed downward. Inhale slightly and, holding the breath in, raise your legs off the floor as high as you can. Use your fists to press down and give you leverage. When you have raised your legs as far as you can, hold this position for a slow count of five.

Now, lower your legs as slowly as you can. It is very important that you do not collapse out of the posture. When your legs are once again on the floor, slowly exhale, unclench your fists and relax for a few moments with your cheek to the side.

The Simple Spinal Twist: Begin by sitting on your mat with both knees pulled up to your chest. The feet remain flat on the ground. The arms hug the legs. Now stretch out the right leg directly in front of you. Place your hands on the floor behind you for support, and cross the left foot over the right knee so that the foot is flat on the ground and the left knee remains high in the air. Take the right arm so that the right elbow hooks over the left knee. Now straighten out the right arm, reach down along the outside of your left leg and foot as far as you are able to, and take hold at some point on the left leg that is comfortable for you. Eventually, you should be able to hold on to the ankle. Remember that your spine should be as erect as possible. Now, keeping the head level, slowly twist your entire body (the head moves with the body) to the left. When you have twisted to your maximum amount, hold that position for a slow count of ten. Remain motionless through this. (See the illustration.)

Next, you are ready to come out of the posture. Slowly let the body untwist, the head moving with the body. Allow your right arm to let go of the left ankle. Bring your right hand back to the ground behind you. Uncross your left leg and bring your right leg up to meet it. Your legs are now in the position they were in at the start of the exercise. Bring your hands around them so that they are once again hugging the legs.

From this point you will simply reverse all the instructions so that you can twist the spine to the right. This posture is complicated to describe, but with the help of the illustration it should be clear to you. Although it takes a while to accommodate the body to it, regular practice reveals that all of the movements involved are actually quite natural to perform.

The practice of Yoga is one way of approaching the human organism as a unified whole. In fact, Yoga is a Sanskrit word meaning "union" or "joining together." Although the physical part of Yoga is approached through the body, the effect of the *asanas* is not limited to physical well being. With regular practice, you will find a recognizable difference in your energy level as well as your feelings about your mental well-being.

And there is something else. Yoga is one of the most accessible ways in which you can become aware that *you are not your mind.* Once you can experience that there is a core of you that is *not* mind, then you can begin to experience what it means to control or expand your mind. It is at once a simple and very complex concept. And it leads to experiences of consciousness that are beyond anything that the mind alone can provide. This is not to downgrade the mind: It is a vital, exciting part of you. But being a part of you, it—like any other part of you—is under your control. This can be a liberating notion.

If you aren't functioning at your optimum, you cannot expect your brain—just as any other part of your body—to be at its best. So some form of regular moderate exercise, as well as good nutrition, should become habitual, as should the avoidance of drugs and alcohol. The brain must receive food energy and oxygen in order to function efficiently, and anything that interferes with that functioning should be avoided.

Some food elements have been found to be associated specifically with development of the brain capillaries. Vitamin E (d-alpha tocopherol), for example, has been shown to rapidly and extensively improve rates of recovery.[1] In addition, except in very rare cases (notably individuals suffering from diabetes), the vitamin has been found to be safe and harmless.

If you decide to take this vitamin, the best way is to gradually increase the dosage. You might start with 30 to 50 international units a day of d-alpha tocopherol and gradually work up to 200 or 400 international units per day. At the same time, a good multi-vitamin might be taken.

Every nutritional element is necessary in some way to the body and therefore to the brain, and much research is being done in this area. It should be noted, however, that some authorities question the value of specific- or mega-vitamin therapy in human nutrition. Certainly, however, you should be aware that if you feed that wondrous machine that is your body a version of garbage, you will not be able to expect it to function at its maximum ability.

General nutritional rules should apply; most importantly, you should make it your purpose never to put foods into your body that deplete nutritional stores. Obviously foods loaded with chemicals and additives should be avoided if possible; fresh, rather than canned foods should be chosen; the ingestion of "empty calorie" foods should be avoided. There are so many natural foods available today that there is virtually no excuse to eat the overprocessed, devitalized junk that so many people settle for. You may feel that you manage fairly well on what you have been eating. Well, see if any of the following statements apply to you:

1. You've just had a checkup, and the doctor says that

you're in fine shape, but you feel vaguely tired a good part of the time, as though you're not functioning quite up to par.

2. You feel somehow as though your life is slipping away from you. You mean to "get organized," but somehow you lack the confidence to reach for the goals that you would like to.

3. Sometimes you feel like crying for no reason at all.

4. Even after a "high-energy" breakfast, you find that you feel somehow sluggish. It seems hard for you to get going, and you feel as though you have to push yourself.

5. Or you feel as though your motor is racing. And because of this nervousness, you can't seem to concentrate on what you need to do.

6. Sometimes after a good meal you can hardly keep your eyes open.

7. Sometimes you find yourself so irritable that you want to break something.

8. You toss and turn at night, unable to lie still much less go to sleep.

9. Sometimes you experience a burst of energy, only to "crash" later on.

10. Sometimes you can't seem to concentrate or focus, and you watch with envy your more goal-oriented friends.

11. Sometimes you experience feelings of distrust towards those closest to you.

Take a moment and look over this list again. Most people have experienced some of the above listed symptoms at some time. Some people have experienced them to alarming degrees. If you, yourself, have been fortunate enough to avoid them, it is almost a certainty that you know someone who hasn't been so lucky.

What causes people to become depressed? What makes people irritable, even violent? Well, the expected answer in our psychologically-oriented modern world is that such people are "neurotic," mentally disturbed to some degree—perhaps even schizophrenic—and certainly in need of some form of psychiatric or psychological care.

As a practicing psychologist, myself, it certainly is not my intention to debunk or criticize the fields of psychology, psychiatry and psychotherapy. Certainly, great gains have been made through the dedicated work of professionals in these related areas. However, it is my premise—and that of a growing number of researchers—that analysis of psychological factors is not sufficient in assessing emotional and mental abnormalities; that the physical state of an individual is sometimes the root cause of a mental disorder; and that mental and emotional disorders can be caused by physical malfunction at the metabolic level.

We tend to think of allergic reactions as being defined by sneezing or breathing difficulties or skin reactions. But the body is highly complex and is capable of subtly reacting to all kinds of things: Foods, chemicals, drugs, stress—any of these can cause difficulties. In addition, for any number of reasons, the body may be unable to create energy normally.

There has been much recent research in this field, a lot of it dealing with hyperactive children. Ben Feingold[2] has been in the forefront of this work, and basically his results seem to prove that some children have marked reactions to artificial coloring and flavoring. These children are prevented from learning and being productive because of the increased activity that their reactions to additives causes, and the simple procedure of removing such chemicals from their diets markedly improves a certain percentage of them without the use of drugs. Simply as a result of removing these additives, these children become able to sit still and concentrate and therefore to learn.

Obviously, if it is possible to extrapolate from experiments done with rats and apply the results to humans, it is possible to extrapolate from work with children that are hyperactive and apply this to adults. Although the physicians—Feingold and William Deamer in San Francisco, William Crook in Tennessee and Mort Teich in New York—have all concentrated most of their work on allergies and hyperactivity in children, Dr. Teich, for one, is finding that some adults also have adverse reactions to food additives and chemicals. In addition, he and others suggest that many adults may have difficulty digesting cows' milk, and that the simple avoidance of milk and milk products may result in a marked difference in physical and mental well-being.

One of the more fascinating aspects of this research is that people react so differently to the same things. For example, certain foods may make one person drowsy, while another becomes hyperactive from the same foods.

The biochemist George Watson has done much research in the field of psychochemical response over a period spanning two decades, and he, too, has concluded that many of the body's functions are directly affected by the foods and chemicals that the body is exposed to. All of these researchers have seen seemingly unexplainable "neurotic" behavior in adults and children be corrected by changes in diet alone. The irrefutable conclusion seems to be that some mental illness is definitely the result of nutritional biochemical malfunctioning.

However, it is very difficult to generalize from their experiences, because a food that will make one person sad or irritable or hyperactive will produce the opposite results in another. Since this is so, it becomes vitally important that each individual learn to detect which foods cause reactions in him. One way to do this is to isolate foods. For example, if you experience some physical or emotional reaction that you suspect may be food or chemical induced, have a meal which consists entirely of that one food. Do not eat anything else for four hours either before or after the test meal. You may have as much of that one food as you want at that meal, but limit yourself to that food alone. If you isolate it in that way, you may be able to tune into your body's reactions to it.

What causes "biochemical reactions" in certain individuals? How does the brain get its energy anyway? The brain and nervous system—just like the rest of the body—depend on the sugar or glucose that is transported in the blood. This sugar is converted into energy by means of a complex process. At different stages of the process, enzymes act as a catalyst to transform the glucose into different amounts of energy at different stages. Since there are so many reactions that need to be completed successfully, and since each reaction depends on how the preceding reaction was completed, it is easy to understand how "any interference with the step-by-step breakdown of glucose in the brain results in impaired mental functioning owing to the incomplete oxidation of glucose intermediates."[3] Where there is "impaired mental functioning," this often results in what looks like mental illness.

What lies at the core of Watson's theory of psychochemical response is the notion that people who exhibit unexplainable symptoms, which are usually thought of as "neurotic," may be divided into two basic psychochemical types: the fast oxidizers and the slow oxidizers. Once an individual's type can be identified, his diet can be adjusted, and he can often be helped.

How about you? Are you functioning at your optimim? If you suspect that you are not, then what do you do? Well, of course, the best course of action would be to locate a physician who is aware of the importance of nutrition in mental performance. But, even without outside help, there is much that the individual can do to help himself.

How do you begin? By noticing and questioning your reaction to any food which precedes any unusual emotional or mental response. If you've just gone through a really low period, instead of putting it down to "holiday blues" or problems you had with your mother when you were five years old, ask yourself what you've been eating.

Obviously this sounds at once simplistic and revolutionary (unless you are among those who are familiar with this notion), but there is enough evidence to indicate that we are, indeed, influenced greatly by what we eat. In this sense, it becomes vitally important to become aware of our own unique responses to foods. It makes absolutely no sense at all to be imprisoned by the concept of a bacon-and-eggs breakfast, for example, if we find that it produces feelings of nausea in us. It makes no sense at all to make food choices influenced by the latest diet fad, or even by what we like. The key lies in choosing foods that like us.

Once again, we are talking about looking at our habitual way of doing things and opening up the possibility that there just might be a better way.

You can do a lot of this on your own. Watson has developed a questionnaire that can aid in determining your psychochemical type.[4] You might consider undergoing a six-hour glucose tolerance test to find out if you are one of those who suffer from low blood sugar or hypoglycemia. It is once again a matter of seeking alternate approaches. One thing that might be helpful is to look back at the end of a particularly energetic day and see what you happened to eat that day; or, if you're dragging around, ask yourself what you ate that day. You might want to keep a record of exactly what you eat for a while (writing things down prevents convenient memory lapses). With this record in hand, you have a better chance of analyzing and evaluating your food reactions. With this new knowledge, you will be able to avoid foods that may be bad for you no matter how "nutritious" they are said to be. Certain foods may be fine for most people, but can be poison if they are eaten by people of the contrasting metabolic type. Fast oxidizers usually react badly to high sugar and starch items like pastries, fruit, ice cream, potatoes, rice and spaghetti. They may also have trouble with lettuce and green peppers as well as milk products and spices such as catsup. Slow oxidizers function badly on sweets that are high in fat content such as cheesecake; vegetables such as avocado; proteins with a high purine content (liver, caviar); and butter (safflower oil seems to be better for them). A slow oxidizer will react well to coffee; a fast oxidizer would do well to avoid it.[5]

You may be definitely in one or the other of these groups. Or you may react differently to different foods depending on the time of the day or the weather. Begin to notice your reactions, so that you can begin to make conscious food choices.

The concept of biochemical type effectively eliminates the concept of "normal." Your nutritional needs may differ considerably from what is considered normal for most people. And, as Watson correctly notes: "The human organism is of almost forbidding complexity when considered from the biochemical—which includes genetic—point of view. There are consequently an untold number of things that can and do go wrong—with genes, with hormones, with enzymes, with nutrition, with infection, with stress, with toxemia and with structure."[6] Understanding this concept provides at least a step toward understanding the possible causes of disturbed behavior which, it must be noted, can sometimes pass for acceptable behavior: Who, but you, sometimes is aware that you are not functioning at your best?

Once again, we have been looking at the need to break down old patterns of viewing things, this time in reference to the nutritional needs of the body. Now let us turn our attention to eye-function itself. In the chapter on communication, in which we discussed speedreading, we addressed ourselves to the need of breaking down old patterns of seeing the printed page. Many of the exercises presented there have a very real value in actual brain improvement because they prevent the eyes from fixating. The normal eye fixes on a point for incredibly brief fractions of a second. If it tries to do so for a longer amount of time, strain results and visual ability is affected.

You actually register most of the information about something in the first instant of looking at it. In fact, if you fix on it long enough, you can reach a point when you literally don't see it at all until you shift your eyes; this is what researchers have come to look at in their study of stabilized images,[7] and in their study of what actually happens during meditation.

From the point of view of good eyesight, therefore, a good habit to form is to consciously shift your gaze, thus stretching and improving your brain's information-handling capacity. By consciously imitating the unconscious shifting that takes place in normal vision, you can bring about measurable improvements in your sight. In addition, shifting also rests the eye.[8]

Here is one way to practice shifting: Look at a word on a page that you are reading. Shift to a word on the same line, but far enough away so that the first word is perceived as less clear. Look at the words alternately for a few seconds. Both words will become clearer and appear to move from side to side in a direction opposite to the movement of the eye. Be sure to blink frequently as you shift.

Your brain receives impressions from all sides, not just from the center of your field of vision. Here is an exercise that will help to awaken and develop your abilities in peripheral vision.

Sit comfortably in a chair and focus on something on the wall opposite you. Be sure that you do not stare. You should blink often during this exercise and simply allow yourself to take in that far point in a relaxed, calm manner. What this actually means is that the eyes will continue their normal continual shifting, although within an incredibly narrow range. Now, continue holding your gaze on this one point, but see how much you can see—at the same time—at the sides of your vision. You must be relaxed to do this. Simply gaze at the point that you have chosen and begin to notice what impressions are coming in from the sides. At first, you will probably only be able to see a blur, but do not let that make you sneak looks to the side. Just relax and see if you can begin to describe what you see at the periphery of your vision.

This procedure needs great concentration and can be tiring, so it is better to break it up into short practice sessions —a few minutes at a time is sufficient. If you do this fairly frequently, you will be able to expand your area of vision.

Once again, we have been talking about seeing in a new way, about breaking down habitual, limited patterns. To improve your brain power by developing your sense of hearing, there are some simple steps that you can take. For example, you might try listening to music from the Baroque period— the Bach two- and three-part inventions would be a good choice. Any situation that you can create in which you train yourself to hear parallel voices at the same time can increase your ability to handle complexity. You might try "tuning in" to two different simultaneous conversations. Work at following the simultaneous lines of sound. Another useful hearing exercise is the listening one that was discussed in the chapter on the smallest chunks of time.

Together with vision and hearing, skill in using the hands and body is one of the best indicators of what kind of physical condition your brain is in. One of the easiest and most pleasant ways to improve dexterity is simply by playing games that provide instant feedback for you. Table tennis, tennis and basketball call upon many different skills, and the fast reactions that they demand provide good training for the brain. Another way to improve dexterity is to do things with one hand that you are accustomed to doing with the other.

The possibilities are endless. As we have seen before, any exercise which transforms your customary, comfortable way of perceiving the world is worth exploring. Remember, as you become more aware, you inevitably experience more control. This, in turn, leads to increased and deepened awareness, which means a more powerful intelligence.

Chapter 16

Motivation and Metamotivation

Why do we set our sights on certain goals? What determines our direction? According to Abraham Maslow, there is a need-hierarchy in which it is hypothesized that an individual only becomes aware of needs higher up as his lower and prepotent needs become more or less satisfied.

You can verify this from your own experience. Just how concerned do you think that you would be with increasing your intelligence if your belly had been empty for a week? It is only as a need is satisfied, that we become aware of the presence of another.

At the lowest level are man's physical and physiological needs. We must have food, rest and shelter or we become consumed by our need for them. Once these needs are somewhat satisfied, they cease to motivate us. It is only unsatisfied needs that act as motivators.

The next need that begins to surface is a need for a certain amount of safety. This is not so much a desire for total security, as it is one in which we can feel relatively free from the possibility of being arbitrarily deprived (as in dependent employment situations, for example).

Once we have achieved relative security, we discover that we also need to belong. Look into your own experience, and you can verify how strong the need is for acceptance by one's peers. We all need to give and receive friendship and love.

These social needs surface as behavior motivators once the so-called "lower" physiological and safety needs are satisfied.

The satisfaction of these social needs leads to the emergence of awareness that we also have ego needs. We become aware of our needs for independence and achievement as well as our desires for status and recognition. Of course, these ego needs usually remain unsatisfied. Once these become apparent to us and important to us, we become insatiable in regard to them.

The need to fulfill the self is the one that emerges last in the hierarchy. "These are the needs for realizing one's own potentialities, for continued self-development, for being creative in the broadest sense of that term. . . . [In the world of reality] the deprivation most people experience with respect to the lower-level needs diverts their energies into the struggle to satisfy those needs, and the needs for self-fulfillment remain dormant."[1]

These need-levels, although listed separately, are actually interrelated and interdependent. Most people tend to be aware of satisfied and unsatisfied areas at each need-level.

This "need-hierarchy" explains to a great extent what it is that motivates us toward certain goals. But what about the self-actualizer? Remember, this is a person who is, by definition, more fulfilled. He has already gratified his basic needs, and one is not motivated by satisfied needs. This is a fascinating concept: If the self-actualizer is already coming from a satisfied base, if he is already secure in his feelings of belongingness and self-respect, if he already feels certain about his place in life, then what motivates him? Once the physiological and safety and social and ego needs are basically covered, what motivates action? What makes the self-actualizer tick? What does he care most about? Is there anything he would die for?

Maslow postulates that the self-actualizer becomes motivated by higher needs, which he calls "metaneeds," and that the self-actualizer becomes motivated in higher ways which Maslow labels "metamotivations."[2]

The importance of the discovery of these "higher" and "highest" values is simply this: Although they are the most vulnerable and least conscious motivators (because they are not basic to sheer survival), they nevertheless do exist. And they exist, not in gods, but in ordinary men. If this is so, then availability of these "highest" values becomes a possibility for all men.

We have talked before about the process of self-actualization. Now let us look at the self-actualizers. What kinds of work are they involved in? In every case, these people seem to be immersed in some vocation that they somehow feel they were destined for. It is a case of "having" to do that which one most "wants" to do. Such people embrace and surrender to the discovery of their fate.

How does one define "work" or "play" in such a context? The words become almost meaningless, since what such individuals enjoy most of all is their "work." What does "vacation" or "rest" mean under these circumstances? And what about the role of money? Money is never a goal in itself for these people; it is always a by-product.

Usually people who are fortunate enough to experience themselves in this way are conscious of feelings of good fortune. It is almost as though they had been "chosen," as though a miracle had occurred. This leads to certain feelings of pride mixed with ones of humility. Of course, they may also feel unworthy, not up to the challenge. As you can verify from your knowledge of the well-known in our society, great success and good fortune can also lead to feelings of alienation and meaninglessness. These are often what come between a man and his ability to experience the highest values.

All right, then, what exactly are these highest values? What are these metaneeds? To what are these people dedicated? It seems that what motivates self-actualizing people are abstract "values" such as truth and beauty, uniqueness, justice, simplicity, efficiency, love, honesty, growth, peace and so on.

These people tend to view their particular professions as instruments through which they can move towards these ultimate values. Here, it must be noted that you cannot form an opinion about whether someone is fulfilling himself or not based only on his profession. People can do the same exact things for myriad reasons and often they are not, themselves, in touch with what actually motivates them. Some women are fulfilled through motherhood, for example; others are not. (I have intentionally used this example, so that you will not think that self-actualization is limited to high-sounding professions.) The key to figuring out if someone is actualizing himself fully lies in the fact that such people regard what they do as an end in itself. It is never perceived as a "job" that is separate from their lives and ultimate identities. And "the closer to self-actualizing, to full humanness, etc., the person is, the more likely [one is] to find that his 'work' is metamotivated rather than basic-need-motivated."[3] In other words, such people become fire fighters in order to create a safe society or protect a community rather than to ensure financial security or status.

In a sense what happens under these conditions is that the self expands to include what would ordinarily be perceived as other than the self. By yearning for these intrinsic values, these people transcend the distinction between the self and the not-self.

Of course, there is no easy way to divide people into those who care about such things and those who don't. Although the average person may work primarily to achieve lower basic needs, probably this is a matter of degree.

If this is so, then *"the full definition of the person or of human nature must then include intrinsic values, as part of human nature."*[4] Most people may be only subliminally aware of these intrinsic values, yet they are potential motivators for everyone. And if we are deprived of beauty or truth or justice or any of the other higher values, we experience deprivations that can be just as painful as that which we experience when any of our other, more basic, needs are not met. Maslow terms these "metapathologies," and they include the boredom and apathy, the feelings of meaninglessness, the fatalism and alienation that so many suffer. The point is that these are real "illnesses" and that they come about directly as the result of our metaneeds being thwarted. Looked at in this way, it can be said that your soul needs beauty just as much as your body needs vitamin C.

This theory provides one way of explaining why there is so much dissatisfaction among those who seem to have everything. Since all their material needs have been met and they are still not happy, they are left feeling empty and bereft.

Many do not realize that there are values *beyond* that they can reach for.

In many ways, of course, we feel ambivalent about these values. We repress these yearnings in ourselves, considering them as "not practical" or "childish," especially since the more basic needs seem so much more important. But these two aspects of man are not mutually exclusive. Man's basic needs exist simultaneously and alongside his metaneeds. The yearning after the eternal verities is just as valid as the need for food.

As we have noticed before, however, these metaneeds often produce feelings of unworthiness in those who are aware of them. Often, too, we rebel against them: Who wants to be good all the time? At this point we come face to face once more with the notion of responsibility to self. When you begin to see your life in terms of your ability and responsibility to choose at various points, you realize that—at least at first—you will have to intentionally become aware of these "higher" needs and encourage and nurture them in yourself. This may mean doing meditation exercises or listening to good music or seeking out experiences and people that will help to move you in the growth direction. Like anything else, the "metalife" only becomes habitual with practice.

When we are functioning at our highest levels, we feel "right" about what we are doing. We feel that it is appropriate and fitting. This appropriateness transcends the separation between what we are and what we want. When we are being motivated by metaneeds, we perceive the fusion between our fate and our free will, and we joyfully embrace our destiny.

If all of this sounds like so much utopian theory, it should be noted that Maslow was no daydreamer. His vision was rather of what he called a "eupsychia." The word comes from the Greek prefix *eu* meaning "good," "easy," "agreeable" and the word "psyche" meaning "the human soul," "the mind," "the intelligence." Eupsychia can thus be taken to mean "moving toward psychological health."[5] It can mean encouraging such movement; it can symbolize an ideal. The word "eupsychian" implies "only real possibility and improvability" rather than notions of "certainty, prophesy, inevitability . . . or confident predictions about the future."[6] Maslow realizes that there is always the possibility that all mankind may be wiped out; but, he reminds us, it is also possible that it *won't* be wiped out. Therefore, "thinking about the future and even trying to bring it about is . . . still a good idea."[7]

How does change come about in a society? As important as any one institution or any particular leader may be, it doesn't take much to realize that merely producing change at that level will not change society as a whole. This is because society is composed of interrelated and multifaceted elements, and therefore true change only occurs over long periods of time when different elements within the society have had a chance to respond to attack. Social change is a slow process.

What kinds of solutions are to be presented when we wish to change society? It should be obvious that there are no simple answers. All we have to do is notice the many new problems that the "solutions" to past problems have created in order to realize that conscious design and planning are necessary—as well as thorough knowledge. It is also helpful if we aim our efforts toward practical goals—institutions and problems upon which we can have some real impact.

All you have to do is look around you to see that change and growth is as possible on the societal level as it is on the individual level. This is a very important statement, and it leads to a stunning conclusion: Once we accept a "slow, holistic revolution by simultaneous attack along the total front, with conscious and controlled knowledge, and infiltration at the weakest or readiest points,"[8] we can learn not to feel disillusioned and disheartened and hopeless and powerless because we can only make a small change in the society as a single person. In other words, if everything above is true, then the "single person is the best there is. That is, one cannot do any more than a single person can do."[9]

The important thing to remember is that what may be involved is a total commitment to hard work at a very low level. Any "cosmic" task is actually millions of small, individual, local jobs that must be done. You may not be asked to give your life for your country; instead you may be asked to run a mimeograph machine. Big, noble-sounding words like "patriotism" and "democracy" boil down to the nit-and-gritty of day-to-day small tasks that must be accomplished as the means to the end.

This does not have to be a discouraging notion, however, because since there are so many tasks and no one person could possibly do all of them, obviously an enormous number of skills will be needed. This leaves the door open for any person to do something that needs doing that he feels like doing. In other words: "Every person can be and should be healthily selfish. That is to say that . . . since every kind of person can be helpful and indeed is needed because he can do things that other kinds of character cannot do, therefore the most unique contribution that he can make is the best contribution that he can make."[10] This is a truly wonderful realization, because it permits us to be "both altruistic and selfish at the same time."[11]

What we are talking about here is the concept of "synergy." Synergy exists, by this definition, when an "individual by the same act and at the same time serves both his own advantage and that of the group."[12] Seen from this point of view, self-actualizers are not selfless, dedicated people, but are rather both selfish and unselfish. And the reason that they can feel so fulfilled about what they are and what they do lies in the fact that their chosen life, what they love most in the world, actualizes them and enriches their lives while—at the same time—it also serves others. As we have noted before, this enables them to transcend feelings of separateness. When people act out of the notion of synergy, competitiveness seems to leave the situation and feelings of cooperation take its place.

If we could truly act out of this concept, we would be in a situation in which we could recognize that we should be thankful and grateful for the contributions that others make. We would welcome the differences between people. Just look around you: There are so many jobs that you either wouldn't want to do or couldn't do. We should come from a position that appreciates that other people are available to do these jobs.

What we have been discussing here is a theory for social improvement. Of course, what is needed to implement it is "a very widespread understanding of the definition of synergy

and of the transcendance of dichotomies which result in synergy."[13]

It is fascinating indeed that this concept for change at the
societal level boils down to the extraordinary importance of
self-education and self-awareness. It is not only for selfish
reasons that you need to look deeply into yourself and expand
your awareness: In order to be able to make your unique
contribution to society, you must identify your best skills and
capabilities. In other words, if society is to grow in a healthy
direction, then each individual has an acute responsibility to
move in the direction of self-development and self-actualization.

Once again, this will mean hard work: The best innate
talent must be cultivated. To move in the direction of self-
actualization means that one is willing to make a commitment.

What about you? Are you willing to put in the work? And
how do you feel about the rest of the world? Do you care what
happens to other people? Well, look closely at the concepts
that I have discussed in this chapter. They are so striking that
they may seem naïve, but within them may lie a way out for
us as individuals and, by extension, for all men and women.
People tend to think that by expanding themselves they must
diminish their neighbor. But, by using the concepts of self-
actualization and synergy, it can be seen that the more the
individual expands the more he can transcend the dichotomy
between the self and the not-self or other. In other words, the
closer you can come to genuine self-actualization, the closer
you will be to making a unique contribution to your world.

Chapter 17

Motivated
Strengths

It is a fact that external data is irrelevant to an individual's sense of self. That is, just as many so-called "successful" people experience themselves as failures as those who are less "successful" in the world's eyes. You have only to notice the number of reported emotional breakdowns among the well-known to verify this for yourself.

How about you? The degree to which you are not getting satisfaction from your life indicates the level at which you probably rate yourself—the old if-I'm-so-great-then-why-aren't-I-rich . . . or happy . . . or . . . you supply the missing word.

Most "experts" advise us to study our mistakes and to learn from these. There is a growing minority, however, that has come to realize that the path to self-fulfillment—unless hit upon by chance—leads through a self-evaluation that emphasizes the identification of a pattern of inner-motivation. These people say that only by identifying and studying our strengths can we take charge of our lives and career development and influence to some degree the course these will follow.[1]

Every individual is unique and does some things better than other things. You may, however, be skilled at certain tasks which give you very little satisfaction. These are unmotivated strengths. This chapter will help you locate your motivated strengths, the skills that recur in experiences that turn you on.

The purpose here is twofold. The exercises suggested here will stimulate your mind, allowing you to tune in even further to the intuitive level of intelligence. In addition, if you take the time to answer the questions thoroughly and honestly, you may discover that you have a revised opinion of yourself, your goals and your plans for the future.

It has been my intention throughout most of this book to discuss techniques that improve intelligence in a such a way that you could fairly easily incorporate them into your daily routine. This chapter differs from the others in that you will have to take some separate time to do the exercises described. You will have to be willing to do some hard work, but I think you will find it exciting. And the rewards are enormous.

Before we begin, however, read the following closely:

"When your purpose is to be a self-actualizing person, the definition of achievement is: 'An experience when you yourself feel you did something well, that you also enjoyed doing, and of which you were proud.' "[2]

Using this definition, almost anything could be considered an achievement. The important aspect here is the satisfaction that you yourself got from the experience. The accomplishment may or may not have counted for much in the world's eyes, but if you personally felt proud of it then it qualifies as an achievement whether it involved saving a life or baking a cake.

Remember, an achievement is "an experience when you yourself feel you did something well, that you also enjoyed doing, and of which you were proud."[3]

All right. Time to begin. You will need some paper, something to write with and, perhaps, some privacy. If you prefer to do this with a friend so that you can get some feedback, fine. You may prefer, however, to work this through alone. Even well-meaning friends can sometimes manipulate choices so, at least initially, it might be preferable to go at this in privacy.

Remember, take your time. You are doing this for *you,* and the more care you take with it, the more accurate your conclusions will be.

It is very difficult to be objective when you begin to look inside yourself. But for the purposes of this exercise, see if you can refrain from feelings of false modesty. Look at yourself from the point of view of a sympathetic observer. And remember, it is of very little value to read through this exercise. You must do it thoroughly, and that means taking as much space as you need. You might consider setting aside a special notebook for this purpose.

All right, then, using the definition of achievement that we have just discussed, begin to list some of the experiences that you have had during which you felt that you were doing well, that you enjoyed and that you felt proud of. Take your time. Since this exercise is meant to spur your memory, don't exclude thoughts that seem extraneous. If you are thinking of something that happened at summer camp and you suddenly remember some other experience that seems irrelevant, take a moment to note down both so that you can come back to each of them.

Here are some questions that may help you to remember specific achievements: Do you have any hobbies? Do you do any volunteer work? Are you involved with any projects outside of your regular work? Are you studying something just "for fun"? What part of the newspaper do you turn to first?

Take your time and list as many of your achievements as you can think of. Describe each one briefly. How old were you at the time? What part of the activity did you enjoy most? Where were you? Don't worry if some of your achievements don't seem as impressive as others. What matters is your feelings about them, not how someone else would rate them. And remember that you can go to any part of your life in choosing achievements to list—personal, professional, community, hobbies, sports, school. Incidentally, feel free to list achievements from when you were very young. Do not monitor or censor yourself in any way.

When you have listed at least twenty achievements, put a check next to the ten that you feel the most proud of, the ones you enjoyed the most. Take a look at these ten experiences and carefully go over them. See if you can locate the skills that you used in order to make them happen. What did you do in that experience? What made it important to you?

Now take a separate piece of paper, and begin to list the various functions or abilities or conditions that were present in these experiences that you have listed as your ten greatest achievements. For example, were you working with other people or were you alone? Indoors or outdoors? Did the experience involve problem-solving? Foresight? Persistence? Did it involve mechanical ability? Creative ability? Were you working with your body? With your mind? Did you have to do research? Speak or write out something? Were you concerned about things or people? Details or overview? Remember, there is no right or wrong about any of this. What you are trying to do is to sift through your experiences to locate those things that you do well that you also like to do, in short, the things that motivate you.

As a foil for this part of the exercise, it might also be helpful if you write down three or four of the greatest disappointments that you have experienced. See if you can isolate out the functions of those experiences. What wasn't there for you? What made the experiences disappointing? What are the things which make you unhappy? See if you can write a detailed answer to that question. Then see if you can separate out which of those things lie within your control, which you are willing to take responsibility for.

Another useful exercise is to write a diary of your life. Where have you been? What have you done? You needn't worry about being chronological or exact. And you can be as exuberant as you like. Try to include what you chose to do in your spare time. Notice where you were and what you were doing when you were having fun. Notice, too, where you were when you weren't.

Now take a fresh sheet of paper and begin to answer the question: Who am I? Answer this question in as many different ways as you can. Do you think of yourself mainly in terms of what you do—writer, lawyer, housewife? In relation to other people—husband or wife, boss or employee? See if you can get beyond these descriptions. Look for alternative answers. After you have answered the question fully, ask again:

Who am I? See what comes up for you. What is your most important identity?

It takes time to answer these questions thoroughly. It takes effort to answer them honestly. By the time you have completed them, you should be closer to identifying those things that you do well and that you like to do; in short, your motivated skills. Knowledge of your strengths provides a bridge to the kind of life that you want.

Chapter 18

Getting What You Want from Life

How do you feel about time? By that I mean, at the end of the day do you have a feeling of satisfaction because you have used the day well? Or is there a nagging feeling that your life is slipping away from you and that you have no control over its direction?

If we are honest and we strip away all of the notions of what we have (possessions and relationships mostly), then we come to the realization that the only thing we ever really have is time. And if we look closely at time, we rediscover the ancient truth that we can never recover past time or capture future time—that the only time we ever truly have is *right now*. You cannot reverse time, and you cannot replace time. When you waste your time, you waste your life.

In this chapter, we will discuss ways in which you can identify those things which are of paramount importance to you, and find the time to do them. Your assessment of yourself, your life and your intelligence will be upgraded significantly as a result of following the suggestions outlined. Once again, though, even if this were not the case, the very doing of the exercises will stimulate you.

The purpose here is not to turn you into a compulsive clock-watcher whose every moment is organized, but to show you how to make the best use of your time. In addition, let me emphasize that I am not talking about *my* judgment of the best use of your time, but *yours.* Everybody has commitments—all those "have-to-do" items in their lives; the aim is to carve out time for yourself so that you get to the things that you *want* to do. Ultimately you are the only one who can truly decide what is most important to you. You are the one who makes the final decision. And it is your responsibility to yourself to make sure that you get to the things that are important to you.

Alan Lakein says that control starts with planning. And what exactly, is planning? Planning is "bringing the future into the present so that you can do something about it right now."[1]

There is no mystery to any of this. It is a matter of (1) locating your goals; (2) setting priorities; (3) scheduling; (4) acting. The interesting thing about all of this is that once you do learn to set priorities, you will have more time just to relax. The more control you exercise over your time the more freedom you gain.

By the way, there is nothing wrong with spontaneity *per se.* It's great to follow impulses and see where they lead us. The problem with living that way, however, is that our time is not limitless. If you want something, you will have to plan to get it or face the probability that you won't get it.

Lakein says that the question which needs to be asked often is: What is the best use of my time right now?[2]

Most people have a very vague notion of time. Oh, they may consult their watches frequently, but basically they forget about all the little chunks of time available to them. They waste precious minutes. Then, too, most people don't think in terms of years, so they don't spend their time *now* in a way that is related to their major goals. Inevitably, this leads to feelings of unfocused frustration. Something is wrong, but they're not sure exactly what.

The solution lies in learning to carve out time for that which is most important. But first you must be able to identify that which is important. In other words, you must be able to identify what you want most in life.

This is getting into a difficult area. It is an area that many people are loath to analyze. But the next few days are inexorably connected to the next few years. Take a moment to let that sink in. It is vital that you come to recognize that what you do today inevitably influences what your tomorrow will be like. You must begin to set your priorities.

Identifying your lifetime goals will give direction to your life. Once you have that, you can begin to deal effectively with everyday problems because they won't overwhelm your main purpose. Knowing what you want to do ultimately will help you to feel in control of your destiny. And it will enable you to resolve conflicts as to how to use your time most effectively.

The following exercise is to be written. Thinking about your goals is not the same at all as writing them down.

The first question to ask yourself is: What do I want most in life? Begin to write immediately; do not think about this too much at this point. Just write out what you want. As you write, see if you can cover all aspects of your life. Include your personal goals, what you want for your family, what you hope to accomplish professionally. Do you have any community goals? Spiritual needs? What about money? Health? Be as expansive as possible as far as areas covered, but limit yourself to writing for two or three minutes at the most. And remember, you're not engraving these goals, you're just writing them down on paper. You'll be able to change your mind if you want to. What about private fantasies? Include everything that you can think of that you want to get out of life.

One of the things that you will discover even at this stage of the exercise is that there are things which are not important to you. Maybe you've always thought they should be, but in terms of what you really want out of life, they don't seem to figure into your scheme of things as high priority items. Just notice this if it comes up for you at this point. Don't try to do anything about it.

Now look over what you've written. Probably a lot of what's there is in fairly general terms. What is necessary now is to begin to focus in more specifically on what you want, so the next question to ask yourself is: If I could plan an absolutely perfect day for myself two years from now, what would it be like?

By putting this question into the future, you should be able to liberate yourself from the strictures of whatever is going on in your life right now. Some people may need to place the question five years away; for some, a year is enough to accomplish this. See how it is for you. See if you can create a day for yourself that is free of shoulds and oughts, and consider that all of the mundane commitments are accounted for. How would it be for you then? Remember, this exercise is not about daydreaming. Write out your answer. Be brief but thorough, and let your imagination create this day for you. Who's going to see this anyway? You can put down anything that you want.

An interesting thing is that people may daydream about being kings and queens, but when it comes down to planning a perfect day for themselves, usually they create situations that are well within the realm of possibility for them. See what comes up for you.

When you have finished this part of the exercise, take a different viewpoint and ask yourself this: What if I knew that I was going to die tomorrow (or six months from now)? What would you do if you knew for sure that your time was limited? Sure, everybody dies, but usually we don't take our own mortality into consideration as we make our daily choices. How would it be if you really knew that you were going to die soon?

. As you answer this question, forget about all the I-would-make-a-will-type answers. That is not what this is about. What you are looking for is those things which you would *have* to do in order for you to feel that you had really lived. The point is to see if there are things that you are not doing now that are important to you.

Some people, answering this question, would choose to continue doing whatever they are doing; others might choose to quit working and travel; others might choose to damn well see if they could write the Great American Novel. There is no right or wrong about this. Just look and see what you would do. Again, don't think too much about it. Start writing.

When you have finished, look over your answers to all three questions. Do they all hang together, or do you find that by suddenly putting a time limit on yourself you have discovered that what seemed important really wasn't and instead you have this other goal that is paramount? Think about what you've written. Does it make anything clearer to you? Remember, that's the whole purpose of the exercise—not to come up with some "right" or high-sounding purpose, but to discover what it is that you specifically want out of life.

Look over your list. If you've really covered many different areas of your life, then you have probably thought of more that you want to do than there is time to do it in. What you need to do at this point is to rank these various goals in their order of importance to you. You don't have to feel bound by any decisions that you make. You can change your mind and readjust your priorities at any time. But you must begin to set priorities, to make choices as to what you are going to do. If different goals seem equally important to you, then acknowledge that that is so for you right now and see—by how much time you allocate to each—which one really is more important to you.

Now go over everything that you have written and choose the ten things that seem the most important to you now as long-range goals that you would like to plan toward. When you have listed the ten most important goals on a separate piece of paper, read over that list and choose the three that are paramount to you. Write these on a separate piece of paper. These three goals represent your choices about what it is you want to do with your life at this time.

There is nothing finite about this. When you look over the three goals, you may discover that they do not genuinely reflect how you feel about your life. Fine. In any event, you should be somewhat clearer about your goals, and that is what this is all about. If the three goals that you have chosen are not accurate, which ones would be? You may want to do the complete exercise again, coming from the perspective that you now have. In any event, you will want to revise any decisions you may have come to periodically as new opportunities and new factors have to be taken into consideration. A good idea at this early stage would be to do this exercise at least twice and compare the results. In all probability you will come up with additional helpful information.

As your life changes, your goals will change, but you need to find out what you want at different times so that you can take action toward fulfilling your goals.

Once you have identified what it is you want out of life, you can complement your long-term planning with short-term planning. What you need to do is to identify exactly what you can do *now* in order to begin to realize your goals. Once again, it is a matter of listing possibilities and then setting priorities.

Notice that I said that what you are looking for is things that you can do now. Do-able activities are different from goals. You set goals to give you something to aim for by locating what it is you want; you then see what you can do to make what you want happen.

With each of your three main long-range goals, see if you can come up with meaningful activities that you are willing to do during the next week or month. What this effectively does is to put you at the level of choice. As you begin to choose, to set your priorities, you begin to feel in control of your life.

> How can you move closer to your lifetime goals? Each day provides a fresh opportunity. Select at least one [high-priority] activity to work on right away and do it. You now have the beginning of an action program for achieving your lifetime goals.[3]

Every day we are faced with all the routine yet essential tasks that we feel responsible for. Unless you begin to take the time for the things that are really important to you, the days will slip away from you and the routine will take over your life. You have to plan to be sure that there will be time for the long-range goals.

I can't emphasize too much here that scheduling is not a matter of arranging your time so that you effectively get everything done which you have to get done. It means making time for the things that you want to do. What you have to get in the habit of doing is planning ahead.

> Remember: *There is always enough time for the important things.* The busiest people are able to find time for what they want to do, not because they have any more time than others but because they think in terms of "making" time by careful scheduling.[4]

What is the most productive time of the day for you? Morning? Afternoon? Evening? When you schedule, see if you can set things up so that you are taking care of the essential things when you are at your best. If you know that your own internal clock runs down at 4:00 P.M., then save that time for opening mail or reading the newspaper.

Be aware of other people's schedules, too. If you know that someone else always plans meetings for the mornings, then save your call for the afternoon or catch him before he gets involved in the day's business.

Remember, too, not to schedule appointments or activities too closely. Leave some time that is unplanned. Set things up so that there is a certain amount of flexibility. You may even want to schedule time in which you do absolutely nothing. Believe it or not, doing nothing can be a very good use of your time. What you are aiming for is not a schedule that has you working all the time, but one that has you working effectively. When you work effectively, a certain amount of time will become liberated so that you are free to do other things. And you might choose, in that free time, to just do "nothing." When you have the time to relax without feeling guilty, you will find that you can return to your work feeling rested and refreshed. You won't be working against yourself, and so you will get more done with less effort and in less time.

With this attitude toward time, what you can do once and for all is effectively eliminate all "waiting time." Any time that needs to be spent either commuting or waiting for another can be a gift to be used either for an activity or a moment of relaxation. It need never be frustrating again. For example, suppose you have decided that one of your goals is to increase your intelligence and you have chosen to use some of the techniques outlined in this book to build your vocabulary as one way to realize that goal. It is a very simple matter to list four or five words, carry them with you on index cards, and make them your own as you "wait" for an appointment. When you take practical steps such as this, you not only move closer to where you want to go, you also end up feeling good about yourself.

In the chapter on memory, we discussed the advisability of not overloading the mind with unnecessary data. That advice is just as applicable here. Instead of planning out in your mind what you will do each day, I would suggest that you write your plans down. Make a list daily—or, even better, each night for the following day—planning out what you must do and what you want to do and setting priorities.

The important point about the list is not that you must complete every item on it, but only that you set priorities and make the best use of your time. Obviously, once you have identified what is most important to you, the best use of your time would be to do that item *right now.*

Keep reminding yourself to focus in on what will bring you the most value. Try to avoid getting bogged down in low-value activities.

Notice that I am not suggesting which activities should take priority for you. There is no "right" about any of this. You are the one who decides the best use of your time. All I am suggesting is that you consciously make decisions and then act on them.

All right, here you are all super-organized and poised for action. But something stops you. What do you do when for some reason you can't tackle that Big Lifetime Goal that you have so neatly identified? The first thing to do is to take another look at your choice. Your reluctance may be based on an intuitive feeling that that goal is not, after all, the best use of your time.

But what if you have a terrific high-priority goal, have validated your choice, and are somehow unable to begin to tackle it? When you find yourself in this kind of predicament, the best way out is to break down what seems overwhelming into small five-minute tasks. It doesn't even matter how large a contribution the doing of such instant tasks will make to the large item. The important thing is to do something—anything—that will get you started on something that is overwhelming. Promise yourself that you will spend exactly five minutes and then stop. Surely you can stand almost any task for five minutes. You may be surprised and find that you become involved after all. But even if this doesn't happen, at least you will have begun.

So far we have been talking about goals—about locating what you want to do and finding the time to do it. But what about learning to tackle the things we *have* to do effectively? The world being what it is, there will always be certain tasks that must be done that are unpleasant: the letters that you don't want to write, the exams that you don't want to study for, the bills that you don't want to pay. The list is infinite. But even as you admit that you must do something distasteful to you, you still have a choice. You can resist it or, having identified it as something that is important to do, you can decide to do it with a positive attitude. You can *choose* to do it. Why make things doubly difficult for yourself? Once you've decided to do something, you may as well give it your best and see if you can get some enjoyment from it.

And if you absolutely can't face it, then learn to procrastinate in a way that will help. The next time you find yourself up against something that you just cannot tackle, see if you can avoid escaping into television or magazines or knitting. Just sit still doing nothing. If you can sit absolutely still for about fifteen minutes without allowing yourself to do anything, a surprising thing will begin to happen; and that is that you should begin to find that you become somewhat uneasy as you realize that something very important to you is not getting done and you're just sitting there doing nothing. Your time is slipping away—and you're doing nothing. It is amazing how effective this method can be in getting you started on something you thought you couldn't face.

Whatever you do, always keep in mind how your present actions might affect your long-range goals. Once you have identified what you want to get from life, keep these goals clearly in mind and remember to go over your list periodically so that you can update it.

Remember that once you have chosen what is most important to you, the best time to do it is now. To spend your time doing anything else, no matter how valuable that might be in its own right, is a relative waste of your time. And remember that to put off a decision is, in fact, to make a decision *not* to do something.

To decide, to be at the level of choice, is to take responsibility for your life and to be in control of your life.

Chapter 19

Problem-Solving

Life can be seen as a series of situations in which, knowing only some of the elements, we must nevertheless make choices. It is the purpose of this chapter to demonstrate effective ways to approach the information that you have in any particular situation, in order to arrive at the most workable solutions.

One of the most surprising results that has come from research in the area of problem-solving is the discovery that people often fail to solve problems because they simply do not use in productive ways the information that is available to them. Often, this is simply a matter of having the patience to work through a given problem in a step-by-step linear fashion.

It has been found, for example, that poor scorers on IQ and similar tests seem to place very little confidence in simple reasoning as a method for problem-solving. Researchers have asked such people to reason aloud and have noticed that, when low scorers don't see an immediate answer to a problem, they give up looking for one. They feel somehow lost and confused. Even though they are able to make most of the correct abstractions and calculations, they fail to use these in ways appropriate to solve the problem.[1]

The problems on IQ tests are usually those of a vertical, logical nature, and these are problems that the mind is very well equipped to handle since the mind habitually functions in a vertical manner, seeking logical solutions to problems.

(And that is why so much of this book has been concerned with breaking down this habitual, rational habit of the mind.)

Since IQ tests normally make use of problems that call upon this reasoning faculty of the mind, it is not really an insurmountable problem to raise IQ scores.[2] (The increasing of total intelligence—as opposed to only that aspect of it measured in IQ tests—is what the rest of the book is all about.)

The most important thing when it comes to raising IQ test scores is simply to start preparing well in advance. You will need to study problems that develop your skill in analyzing information and reconstructing relationships. These are information-processing skills that can be developed with practice. There are many books available with sample questions of IQ, SAT or similar tests, and if you practice on old tests, you can improve your score on the new tests.

The important thing about approaching these tests is to *read the instructions carefully,* and keep yourself from jumping to conclusions about what the solution might be until you have looked for it in a step-by-step fashion. It helps, with this kind of problem, to think aloud; this often will keep you from losing the patience necessary to solve these problems. Remember, such problems usually require little formal education; what is necessary is patience and a reasoning-through of the available data.

It can be helpful if you can arrange to have feedback during your work. Ideally, this will mean working with a qualified tutor or a small group; but most books that contain old tests also supply the answers to the questions so there is much that you can do on your own.

Very often, though, the step-by-step approach just isn't enough when it comes to solving problems, because what is necessary is looking at all the available data and arranging it in a different way; that is, restructuring it. I will discuss this aspect of problem-solving in more detail in a later chapter in which you will be able to learn some ways that specifically encourage generative thinking. (This is a horizontal approach to problem-solving as opposed to the vertical one that we have been looking at here.)

For the moment, though, my intention is to give you some

general suggestions about looking for solutions to problems.

An important point to note about problems, and one that you can verify from your own experience, is that usually once a solution has been stated, it is perceived to have been "obvious." If this is so, then why is it that sometimes we labor over the finding of it?

Well, sometimes this is simply a matter of rearranging the known facts in a problem. If you can come at them from a different perspective, you may be able to put the available data together in a different way.

Remember that the mind functions normally in a vertical, step-by-step manner. If you begin your search for the solution to a problem by collecting the wrong elements, you may still find a solution; but you should realize that the order in which you place the elements will influence any conclusion you come to. If you have a faulty foundation, you may end up with an inappropriate construction.

About the only protection you have against going in the wrong direction when it comes to solving problems is to try several approaches. As long as you don't get stuck in any one way of looking at the problem, you stand a much better chance of eventually finding the optimum solution. This is simply because there is no way to guarantee that any one approach will furnish the "right" answer.

What follows are some suggestions that you should find helpful when looking at problems. Each of these suggestions involves concrete actions that you can take to help you in the problem-solving process.

1. See if you can note (either mentally or on a piece of paper) all the elements that comprise the problem. Once you have identified everything that you believe to be involved, run all of these elements over in your mind rapidly. Do this several times and see if some sort of pattern seems to emerge. If you keep all of the elements in mind, at first, you will have some protection against getting stuck on just a few of them and forgetting the total picture.

2. See if you can avoid coming to conclusions for a while. Judgments and evaluations tend to prevent us from seeing new ways to structure available information.

3. Try rearranging the elements that you have listed.

Since the mind works in a vertical manner, the information that happens to come in first influences any conclusions that we come to. See what happens when you change things around.

4. Don't allow yourself to feel trapped by any direction that you happened to take. Constantly be on the lookout for new combinations. Remember that often solutions appear suddenly, so relax and keep yourself open to the possibility that one will come.

5. As you reason, be critical of your ideas. Come at them as objectively as you can, looking for their weak points. At the same time, be constructive when you evaluate the ideas of others, looking for the strong points in their solutions. What this does is to create an atmosphere and an attitude that will be constructive to the problem-solving process.

6. Try changing the form of the problem. If the problem is verbal, see if you can make it concrete by drawing a graph or making a model. If you already have a concrete form, then see how it looks as an abstraction.

7. If you come to a dead end, then take a complete break from what you are doing. Remember, though, that if that approach genuinely represented a fruitless direction, it will do you no good at all to come back after your rest and begin where you left off. The better way would be to try a fresh approach.

8. See if talking helps. Remember that when you communicate with another you will, of necessity, have to be clearer in your own mind in order to make your problem understandable. Also, often the feedback provided by another person will help you to locate inconsistencies in your reasoning.

These are all commonsense rules. In addition, here are some other things that you can do when approaching a problem.

1. You have learned the value in writing various elements down, as opposed to trying to think things through. This idea is invaluable in tackling problems. Just by listing and setting priorities, solutions may begin to appear to you.

A variation of this suggestion is the use of *brainstorming*, which refers to a technique originally developed in business planning conferences in which ideas and suggestions are offered in an unrestrained and uncritical manner by all members of a group. This method very often yields sudden inspiration-like or cognitive rearranging of the available data, and it can be applied on an individual level.

2. Some problems fall into the ". . . but" category. That is, they are of the order of "I want to do this *but* I have to do that." An astonishing thing happens if you merely substitute the word "and" for the word "but." By stating the problem as "I want to do this *and* I have to do that," you suddenly find that you are free to choose your priorities.

3. See what part of the problem you can be responsible for. Obviously, if you feel that somebody is "doing it to you," then how can you do something about it? By locating what contribution you make to the problem, you will be able to discover areas in which you can contribute to the solution.

4. See if you can give up the idea of being right—at least for the moment. Sometimes the solving of a problem necessitates your doing something that you "shouldn't" have to do.

Let me stop here and give you an example of what I mean. A couple that I know are separated. The husband is now out of town and has asked his estranged wife to pick up mail weekly at his mother's house. This is necessary because checks will arrive that he doesn't want left there. His wife was at first angry and resentful. They're separated, aren't they? Why should she be responsible for this? After all, the man has two brothers who certainly should be taking care of these things. The woman was very aware that she was right that the man should have made arrangements before he left town. As long as she was focused on being right, she saw no way out of her dilemma. Her husband had all kinds of reasonable and rational explanations as to why she was the only available person who could help him, and her schedule was such that a forced weekly trip of over thirty miles was something that she did not relish.

Suddenly, she stepped back and decided that being right wasn't helping her find a solution to the problem. As soon as she gave up the idea of being *right,* it occurred to her that she could have the mail forwarded directly to her. Of course, that's an "obvious" solution. I can only say that it didn't occur to either of the people involved in the problem as long as each was intent on being right.

5. The example just given also illustrates the following point to a certain degree. Very often, the reason that we cannot locate the solution to a problem is simply because we haven't correctly defined it. A good part of the solution to any problem lies in the correct definition of it.

6. This suggestion has to do with the concept of choice. We tend to think that our choices come as a result of our considerations and things we must take into account regarding some matter. This is not correct. Choice is something that comes after consideration and comes about only after we get our considerations out of the way. So, when you have to choose, look carefully at all your considerations: Analyze them thoroughly; put them behind you; and then and only then, choose. Somehow, once you have your considerations out of the way, it becomes much easier to choose.

For example, I know someone who was asked to take care of a friend's dog while his friend was away. This may seem like a simple request, but for this person (whom I'll call Bill), it was a dilemma. Bill likes his friend and wants to help him out, but he has all sorts of considerations about dogs: They have to be walked; they dirty up the streets; they get in the way and dirty the house, etc. As long as he focused on his considerations, he was unable to choose what to do. As soon as he faced and analyzed his considerations, he was able to freely choose what he *wanted* to do. It doesn't matter what he eventually chose. The important point is that after you have noted that you have this consideration and you have that consideration and you have this other consideration, you are then free to choose what you will do.

7. We have discussed before the notion of the here-and-now. We have noted that self-actualizers function in the present moment. This approach to life is the same one that you should take to the problem-solving process.

The best way to view a present problem is to give it your undivided attention. By studying its unique nature, you will be able to discover, within the problem itself, the elements necessary to the solution. Remember, when solutions are missed, it is usually because people simply do not make use

of the information that is available to them. By focusing completely on the problem and having the intention of finding a
solution, you greatly increase your likelihood of doing so.

Any other way is often a matter of applying experiences and
habits and knowledge from the past to the present situation.
Sometimes this works because the present has similarities to
the past; but the present is distinct from what has gone before
and should be considered in its own right.

The past is only helpful when it is active and alive and has
been absorbed into the present person. It is not something
that can be used and reused. A meal that you have eaten
cannot be eaten again. In the same way, when you approach
a problem, approach it as a whole person whose past is certainly a part of you, but who is not limited by that past from
finding new solutions.

One final point. As you approach any problem, your own
mind-set can have an astonishing degree of influence on how
successful you are in dealing with it. If you see it as a negative
experience, it will be more difficult to deal with. Since you
view it as an important task, you might as well embrace it as
an exciting challenge, and yet another opportunity to expand
your mental capabilities.

———◄◆►———

Chapter 20

Horizontal
Thinking

So far, in our study of the mind, we have found it convenient
to divide the ways of thinking into two contrasting modes. We
have considered the mind from its logical aspect and discussed some ways in which to increase intelligence through
better use of this aspect; and we have talked about the more
intuitive, creative aspect of mind and explored some of the
ways in which it is possible to tap into this mode of thinking.
In a sense, we have been looking at ways to expand by going
deeper into ourselves, noticing that the more aware we are of
what is going on within, the more able we become to expand
in all directions.

There is another way of approaching this logical-intuitive
dichotomy of mind, however, and that is to think of the two
modes of thinking as being vertical and horizontal. In other
words, logical is to vertical as intuitive is to horizontal.

As we have seen, it is possible to tap into deeper levels of
awareness and to set things up for ourselves so that we are
receptive to cognitive and insightful experiences. Horizontal
thinking represents a practical tool that we can use in order
to encourage and generate ideas in such a way that the information that is already available to us can be restructured and
rearranged.

Why do we need this other way of thinking? Very simply,
because—as we have discussed before—the logical and ratio-

nal cheats us out of a whole range of experiences. And—again, as we have seen before—that aspect of the mind is so efficient that we very easily become trapped by it. Once we have found what makes sense to us, once we have come upon a solution that works for us, we tend to automatically reject anything else. But the truth is, that although we may have found an adequate solution, we may not have found the *optimum* solution.

The logical aspect of the mind is very valuable, but it is limited. With logic it is easy to add to existing information, but it is difficult to restructure information—to be able to come at things freshly, to get a new perspective. And of course that is where insight and creativity come in, because both of these are a function of seeing things in a new way.

Many of the exercises in this book will enable you to tap into this reservoir of power on a more regular basis. The advantage of considering this creative aspect as horizontal, however, is that horizontal thinking can be approached in a logical way; that is, you can learn techniques—practical things that you can do in order to think horizontally. You can learn to approach problems with an attitude that enables you to escape from the limitations imposed by vertical thinking.

Part of the fun in looking at things in this way is that horizontal thinking allows you to give up being right all the time. This is because the main function of considering information in this way is simply to generate ideas, whereas vertical thinking restricts you to being right at each step along the way. Let me explain what I mean by that. Vertical thinking is something like building a sound foundation and adding blocks on top of it as you go. When faced with a problem, the way that we usually approach it is to go step by step with it, logically moving from one level to the next. We may or may not have an insight along the way, but basically we do not move on to a level until we are certain that we have been right up to that point at least.

If we approach a problem with the attitude implied in horizontal thinking, however, we will suspend judgment for a while and follow impulses wherever they lead—just to follow them. Horizontal thinking complements vertical thinking. It doesn't take the place of it. But it is a very specific way to become skillful at generating new ways of looking at things; in short, a practical and deliberate way in which to encourage creativity.

Take a moment to study the following characteristics implied by each of these ways of approaching information. By contrasting the two in this way, I intend to underscore the distinctions between them. If you take the time to understand these thoroughly, you will be able to begin to take on the attitude necessary to thinking horizontally.

Vertical Thinking	*Horizontal Thinking*
Selecting	Generating
Having the right answer	Having a rich assortment of alternatives
Finding the right direction	Generating a direction
Analyzing	Provoking
Moving in sequence	Jumping around
Being right at every step	Not being concerned with being right along the way
Excluding the irrelevant	Welcoming instrusions
Classifying and labeling	Not being concerned about labels
Seeking the most likely	Exploring the least likely
Coming up with a solution of sorts	Having the chance to come up with an optimum solution through insight, but allowing for the possibility of not finding a solution at all

By now you no doubt have an understanding of what is meant by the distinction that has been made in these two forms of thinking. But, as I have emphasized throughout this book, understanding is only a beginning. You need to be able to experience this distinction, and you need to be able to use specific methods so that you can encourage this kind of thinking in yourself.

One of the most important tools at your disposal when

approaching information is your attitude toward it. With the attitude implied in thinking horizontally, you simply look at any particular way of seeing things as just one possible way of structuring that information. You accept the usefulness and convenience of that particular pattern, and then you look for new ways of structuring the information, simply in order to see how it will look some other way.

In other words, you needn't be looking for a better way in order to challenge the old way. You needn't be looking to prove the old way either right or wrong. It is simply a matter of wanting to take a fresh look at things, of avoiding rigidity simply to avoid ridigity. The attitude implied in horizontal thinking means always trying to see if there are alternatives, other ways of structuring things. Anything goes in this way of thinking except holding on to some solution—any solution.

The most important general principle underlying this way of looking at things is that information can be looked at and considered for the effect that it will have rather than for any intrinsic value it has in and of itself. What this means is that you do not have to concern yourself with reasons and justifications in order to use a piece of information. What concerns you is only the effects that might follow from using the information. For example, you might choose to throw a random word into consideration of some problem just to see what ideas it would generate.

One of the most important uses of horizontal thinking is the value it has in problem-solving. Many problems need only more information or better techniques to lead to solution. For these, vertical thinking does very nicely. But where a rearrangement of available information is necessary, horizontal thinking is required. There is another kind of situation which requires horizontal thinking: This is when we have a solution that seems adequate to us. In order to open the possibility of finding a much better one, we have to break out of our comfortable, habitual way of looking at the information.

In this chapter, I will introduce you to some of the techniques that you can use in order to practice thinking in this way. What is necessary is that you practice thinking horizontally so that you can get into the habit of thinking in this way.

Edward de Bono uses geometric figures in order to introduce the practice of what he calls "lateral thinking."[1] This is because there is nothing equivocal about a visual figure. In other words, as contrasted to verbal material, there are no individual shades of meaning that are presented with visual figures. By starting with geometric figures, you are able to grasp the concept of thinking in this way on an experiential level, without becoming muddled in the ambiguities of words. With words, you would probably move back and forth between vertical and horizontal thinking. By restricting your beginning practice to geometric figures, you can clearly distinguish between the two processes.

In describing the geometric figures, remember that your main purpose is to generate as many different ways of looking at them as possible. There is no right or wrong about this. See if you can suspend judgment. Do not reject any idea because it seems "silly." Any alternative is a viable alternative. There is only one limitation: In describing the presented figure, do not describe what the figure could be or what it reminds you of. What you are being asked for is "an alternative description" of it, phrased in such a way that someone else would be able to re-create the figure based upon your description of it.

For example, how would you describe the following figure?

There are several alternatives. You might see it as two squares joined by a connecting line. Or you might see it as a line with a square at each end. Another way of looking at it would be as two squares with short tails that are placed so that the tails are in line. You might even see it as four half squares, two placed on top of the other two as in the illustration at top of next page.

Of course you might say that seeing the figure as "two squares joined by a line" is the same as seeing it as "a line with a square at either end." The important thing about seeing it one way or the other, however, is that in one case your atten-

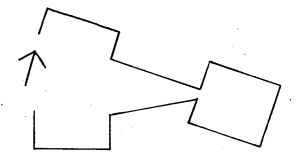

tion is centered on the squares and in the other case your attention is centered on the line. "From the point of view of what happens in the mind, the sequence of attention is of the utmost importance hence a different sequence of attention is a difference."[2]

What about the following figure?[3]

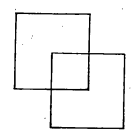

You could see it as two overlapping squares or as three squares. You might see it as a square gap surrounded by two "L" shapes. Or you might say that it represented a rectangle that has been pushed out of line.

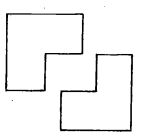

Notice how things open up as you begin to consider the possibility of other alternatives. At first you may find that the obvious pattern is all that you see; but as you begin to consider that there are alternative ways of looking at the figure, you will begin to see them. And sometimes just a slight shift of attention will make a huge difference in the way something is put together.

By now, you probably have a much clearer idea of what is meant by horizontal thinking. Now, how does this translate to verbal uses? Well, one way is to study pictures and written material in such a way that you try to understand the point of view of each person involved. You don't have to agree with the various points of view. The purpose is simply to practice looking at a situation from other points of view. See, also, if you can avoid trying to prove one point of view superior to another; that is not the point of the exercise. But (as we have seen in the chapter on communication), an "advantage of being able to put forward an opposing point of view is that one then has much more chance of restructuring it."[4]

One of the most valuable tools available when coming at verbal information in a horizontal way is to allow yourself to question it. You do this by asking: Why? You question, with this technique, even if—and especially when—you already have the answer. In other words, your purpose here is not to explain something unfamiliar in familiar terms, but rather to question even the familiar terms. For example, you might ask yourself why people have five fingers; or why typewriter paper is usually sized 8 1/2" × 11"; or why wheels are round. In doing this exercise, you simply ask the question "Why?" You then offer an explanation, which you answer with another Why? and so on. This is something like the questioning that children do of everything, but it is important to refrain from a mechanical "because" answer. The whole idea is to show that no assumption is so sacred that it cannot be challenged.

Another valuable tool that we have touched on in regard to horizontal thinking is that of holding off judgment. We usually evaluate very quickly, applying judgment as to whether an idea is relevant or valid or correct. But interesting things happen when you delay judgment. For one thing, ideas stay around longer and may generate further ideas. As inhibitions about "being wrong" are removed, ideas that might have been rejected out of hand can be introduced and may prove useful. Then too, ideas can be looked at as possible sources of stimulation rather than being rejected because they couldn't conveniently fit in at the moment. And ideas that might have been judged absolutely wrong may survive long enough to prove themselves right in the end.

Another way of thinking horizontally involves intentionally turning things around or upside down or inside out. In other words, you reverse the information—not to prove anything, but just to see what will happen. Reversing information may provoke new ways of looking at it and can lead to ideas that otherwise would not have been accessible. Even if reversing the information leads to something that makes no sense whatsoever, you may still get value out of looking at it in this way. This is true because anything that you can do to see something in an alternate way means that you are opening up possibilities of breaking out of old patterns, and this in itself may lead to new ideas.

By reversing the information, you may reach a viable solution. All well and good, but that is not the main purpose. Mainly, you reverse something simply to see what will happen. If nothing is gained, well, nothing is lost either. And just challenging your habitual way of looking at something is valuable in and of itself.

In this chapter, my intention has been to introduce another tool to you that would enable you to reach further into your own abilities. The most important point to remember is a simple one to understand but a difficult one to put into practice: It is that in approaching a problem or a picture or information of any kind, if you approach it horizontally you will be seeking to generate a different way of looking at it rather than seeking to come up with the right way of looking at it. Anything that you can do to achieve this end is of value and should be considered not for what it is in itself but for the effect it has on the situation.

In order to acquire skill in looking for alternate ways, you must practice approaching information horizontally. Once again what is important here is a disruption of the easy, the comfortable, the acceptable, the habitual. The breaking down of the barriers imposed by rigid patterns leads to an expansion of awareness and a deepening of experience; in short, to an increase in intelligence.

———— ◄ ► ————

Chapter 21

What To
Do About Fear

It has been my purpose throughout this book to fuse the two streams of learning in such a way that it would become comfortable for you to reach into either sphere depending upon your particular needs of the moment.

Some of my instructions may have seemed contradictory, since often you were instructed to approach new learning in a systematic, rational and commonsense way, while at other times you were asked to suspend logic and allow your more intuitive intelligence to act.

However, if studied as a whole it can be seen that my approach is consistent throughout and is predicated on a holistic approach to creativity.[1] Creativity, according to this view, is not something that happens on a particular day of the week and only in special surroundings. On the contrary, it can be an aspect of practically any behavior at all. And, at the same time, if we wish to improve in a certain area, the best way to achieve this successfully is to seek improvement in other areas, most importantly those of self-knowledge.

This can easily be demonstrated. For example, if we decide that we would like to improve our writing ability, we can do this to a certain extent by studying writing technique at some school. Of equal importance, however, will be anything that we can do to enable ourselves to become more free about ourselves, less inhibited, etc. This, in turn, can easily be seen to be related to our feelings about ourselves in other areas. So that, if we want to improve our writing ability, a good place to start would be any area that would lead to self-awareness and self-knowledge.

What are the things that hold us back from this knowledge? Well, one thing that does is our fear of the illogical and irrational within us—that "crazy" and childlike part of us. But what is this part of ourselves that we try to suppress? If we look objectively at it, it turns out that it is that within us which is most creative.

What I am saying is that when one studies creative people, or people that Maslow calls self-actualizers, one finds in them —to a heightened degree—those very qualities which the sensible world finds most troublesome. After all, the creative person basically is not satisfied with the world as it is; he wants to make another world. However, every human being has within him "both rational and nonrational, both child and adult, both masculine and feminine. . . . We lose by trying daily to be *only* and *purely* rational . . . *only* sensible, *only* practical, *only* responsible."[2]

By the way, I am not implying that creativity is always to be preferred over common sense. One thing that is often overlooked is that you cannot live for the peak-experiences alone. That moment of cognition or insight is just that—a flash, a tiny fraction of the time that we have. The rest is hard work. It takes a lot of hard work after the bright idea to make it come to fruition. What is often forgotten is that the people who create also have to be good workers.

By and large, we want airplanes to take off on time and our mail to be delivered, and nobody wants a creative doctor who will try something new on him. But what I am saying is that the rational is very different from the cognitive and that the healthy individual fuses these two aspects of his personality.

This is why I have suggested ways for you to break down the barriers between what you are and what you could become. The healthy, creative—and truly intelligent—individual is able to transcend the dichotomy between his intuitive and rational natures. He can voluntarily call upon the child within him to fantasize, and he can then bring his fantasies into the world of reality. He is available to himself at all levels.

I have shown you many ways to tap into your more intuitive powers, and I have indicated practical exercises to improve on both levels of intelligence. What I intend to discuss now is some of the ways that you can deal with the fears that will surface. Once again, let me emphasize that all of the chapters in this book indirectly will aid you in dealing with fears and insecurities. Some do this by giving you information (we tend to be afraid when we feel unsure in some area), and some do this by putting you in touch with your deeper feelings (once feelings are in the open, they can be confronted). And, as I said before, anything that will expand self-knowledge will lead to improvement even if the desired area of improvement is not specifically being worked on at the time.

In addition, it has been my intention all along to encourage you to—and to demonstrate methods by which you can—function in the here-and-now, in the present moment. When you are totally absorbed in some activity, you tend to become less conscious of yourself automatically. You are less apt to be observing yourself in a critical way. You come closer to experiencing rather than understanding. "This kind of self-forgetfulness is one of the paths to finding one's true identity, one's real self, one's authentic nature."[3]

This is all well and good, but sometimes—despite all that we know—we are still encumbered by very real fears, and there are some simple, conscious steps that we can take to overcome them.

First, begin by arousing your enthusiasm for what you are about to undertake. Your chances of success in any area are strengthened immeasurably when you are going in the direction that you want to go in. So if you have decided to do something, make that thing important and interesting to you. Your enthusiasm will be communicated to others.

Second, know your subject thoroughly. It is easy enough to verify for yourself that on those occasions when you were really secure about something, your confidence was enhanced to a significant degree.

Third, act confident. This is not a casual suggestion. As William James has noted, action seems to follow feeling, but really the two go together. And by regulating action, which is under more direct control of the will, you can indirectly regulate the feeling, which is not.

Obviously, if you are not prepared, your act will not fool anyone—least of all you. But if you are enthusiastic and thoroughly prepared, your assumption of confidence can help lead you to the feeling of confidence.

Fourth, practice a lot. It is the unknown that frightens us. If you do something until it becomes habitual, it no longer looms as unapproachable simply because of its very familiarity.

What is it that enables some people to succeed where others fall short of their goals? To me, the answer is twofold. The first part has to do with the fuzzy way in which most people look at their goals. It has been my strong intention in these pages to help you focus in on what you really want. Obviously, you can't go after something single-mindedly until you are sure that you want it.

The second part of the answer to the question of why people don't reach their goals has to do with the fear of failure. The monster that is failure is so uncomfortably frightening that often we would rather not try at all than risk confronting it.

Well, let me tell you a story that you may not be aware of. Everybody knows the legend of the great Babe Ruth and his fantastic record of home runs. But what many people don't know is that the great Babe struck out more times than any other player in history. He *failed* 1330 times! And don't forget that when Ruth struck out he did so in full view of a jeering crowd.

If you believe in yourself and in what you want to do, you have to face the fact that your chances of success will be directly proportional to the number of times that you are willing to go to bat. Yes, every time you do try you could fail. But the more times you are willing to risk failure, the more likely you will be to eventually succeed. Take a moment and think about that. It is a truth that is very easy to forget: How much more comfortable to blame events over which we have no control instead of looking to ourselves and realizing that much of success is just plain, unvarnished persistence.

Another good word for persistence in this context is indifference. Once again we are talking about that self-forgetfulness that Maslow mentions. When you are not concerned about what other people will think, you can be at your best. Today's failure won't matter in the long run, unless it makes you quit. Individual failures mean nothing at all if you succeed eventually. And each time you try you get better at what you are working towards, so that one day that which now seems impossible will be within your grasp.

Here are some steps that you can take to bypass your fear. They are not intended to cure you of emotional problems, but simply to allow you to function until you can work your problem through.

First, ask yourself: What am I afraid of? Then, write out a list of possibilities and single out the most likely culprit. Very often, exposing your fears can make them containable.

Second, ask yourself: What is the very worst thing that could happen? If you allow yourself to answer this honestly, you can exaggerate and blow up your fear as much as you like, admiting to every ridiculous fantasy. Once again, just the doing of this can help.

My last suggestion for dealing with fear is that you encourage yourself to experience it. Take a moment, close your eyes and take a look at your fear. Describe it to yourself. Is it located in a particular place in your body? Your throat? Your gut? Your back? Where, exactly? What color is it? What shape? Could you pour it into a pint-size container? Quart-size? How big?

Is your heart pounding? Are you sweating? Just look. Observe what the fear feels like and what it smells like and what it looks like. As you observe, you may find that it changes its form. Once again look at it closely. It is very important that you not try to deny it or to manipulate it. Just watch as your hands shake and that lump in your throat prevents you from speaking.

It is not possible to translate these words into the experience that you will have if you actually follow the steps outlined above. By permitting yourself to experience your fear, by not denying what is going on with you, you can open up space for yourself that was not there before.

No one can totally eliminate fear, but you can learn to push through it and not let it stop you from achieving eventual success.

——◄◆►——

Chapter 22

About Trying
and Doing

Have you ever seriously considered why people fail? I don't
mean all the reasons and excuses and people we blame for
preventing us from living up to our expectations. I mean
seriously looking at what keeps us from fulfilling our potential. If you look honestly enough, you may discover a surprising fact: Namely, that along with the will to live and the will
to achieve that is in all of us, there is also something quite
sinister—a *need to fail.*

But how absurd, you say. Why should anyone *want* to fail?
Because, very simply, failure can be a very seductive thing.
For one thing, think of all the hard work the failure avoids:
Remember that all of the self-actualizers that Maslow studied
were hard workers. There is also the company of most of the
rest of the world. People often feel threatened by individuals
who are fulfilling themselves, so we save ourselves from being
the butt of much gossip and negative feeling by removing
ourselves from the contest. Another thing: If we ourselves are
not out there doing and acting, we can fantasize how much
better we *could* do whatever it is than those who are actually
engaged in the work; we never have to face the possibility of
our real efforts not measuring up to our dreams. I could go
on and on, but I believe that you can begin to see what I mean
when I say that the rewards of failure can be very tempting.

However, in our understandable need to shun the possibility of pain and humiliation and disillusionment, we do something to ourselves that, if we looked objectively at it, would horrify us: Namely, rather than face the possiblity of failure, we do not act at all, thereby guaranteeing failure. What I mean is, although it is true that if we act we might come up short, it is equally true that if we *don't* act, we *surely* will. The result of this avoidance is that we insure for ourselves far greater pain than we have avoided—and at the cost of an enormous expense of energy.

Because—contrary to what you may think—it takes energy to be a failure. It takes an enormous amount of energy to think up excuses and reasons and people to blame for making us less than we hoped we would be. It takes energy to fill up our lives with wasteful activities in order to avoid that which is most important to us.

And the truth that we lose sight of continually is just this: One small accomplishment in the real world is worth a mountain of "I could have's" and "if only's." Satisfaction lies in completion, in doing what we ourselves have chosen to do, and all of our dreams and fantasies cannot take the place of seeing some small achievement in the world of reality.

Notice here that I have not defined success by some rigid formula. As we have discussed before, only you know what it is that you should be doing, and only you know if you are fulfilling your potential.

But since all of us are, to some degree, victims of the need to fail, how do we get out of our own way? Well, that is what this book is all about, and in this chapter I would like to share with you a formula about success that I came across some years ago and which I have come to see as one of the quickest and most effective tools we can have on our way to self-actualization. It is a formula that is so simple that it may be difficult for some to accept its power. But since using it brings almost immediate results, you can easily verify it for yourself.

It is simply this: Act as if your success were virtually assured.

Before your mind begins to come up with objections, let me assure you that I am not advocating that you hypnotize yourself or repeat slogans to yourself stating that you cannot fail. This formula has nothing at all to do with hypnotism, although one aspect of hypnotism may give us some insight into how and why it works.

When someone is hypnotized and does something that he previously was unable to do, it is not that he has magically acquired new abilities, but simply that he is in a state of consciousness in which he is not considering the possibility of failure. What this does is to release the abilities that he always had but were unavailable to him because of fear and considerations on his part. In the same way, when you act as if your success were virtually assured, what you do, in essence, is just to propose to yourself the question: What if . . . ? What if it were really impossible for you to fail at whatever you have in mind (traveling around the world, learning a language, going back to school, moving to a new town, writing a book—whatever)? What would you do, exactly? What action would you take, specifically? What would be your first step? Whatever it is—do that.

By taking that first step, you absolutely move your goal outside of the realm of fantasy and into the world of reality. Now ask again: What would I do if my success were virtally assured? Just suppose for a moment that this is true. And then take this next step and the next and the next. Before you know it, you may achieve your goal. At the very least you will, with certainty, be moving toward it.

What we are talking about here is very much related to what many philosophers and some psychologists mean when they talk about "trust" as opposed to "trying," of the feeling of acceptance that seems to coexist with the creative attitude.

> In moments of here-now immersion and self-forgetfulness we are apt to become more "positive" and less negative. . . . [This implies] a kind of trust in the self and a trust in the world which permits the temporary giving up of straining and striving, of volition and control, of conscious coping and effort.[1]

Total concentration, as we have learned in our meditation and other mental exercises, is *not trying.* It is a process in which the mind no longer judges what we are about, so that we are free to act because we are no longer controlled by our fears. If you know where you want to go and you stop analyz-

ing all the how's and why's, you will find that you automatically move in the right direction. We see this quite easily
either walking or driving a car. All it takes is the thought that
we want to move in some direction, and, sure enough, we do.
The more we stop and consider and try to figure out consciously which foot to move first, the less likely we are to
actually move and the more complicated things become.

The rest of life is exactly the same, although we make it
complicated. If you want to do something, then take a step
toward doing it. What we have to allow ourselves to grasp is
the fabulous notion that when we actually move forward,
though the movement be infinitesimal, we have not failed to
reach our goal; we have simply not reached it *yet.* And each
movement that we make in the world of reality brings us that
much closer to accomplishing just what we set out to do.

So often we spend precious moments of *now* deciding that
we really could have done better at something if only things
had been different, when the simple truth is that if we could
have done better, then we would have. In other words, no
matter what excuses we come up with, the simple fact is that
what we do at any particular moment is the best that we could
have done *then.* However, having had that experience, we are
now better equipped, and our next action will be closer to the
mark.

Once a goal has been set, a common misconception that
many people experience is the notion of trying and failing to
reach that goal and perhaps, eventually, succeeding. This is
a pitfall: *You either do or you don't do.*

If you have set a goal of running four miles and you run one
mile the first day, then you haven't failed to run four miles
that day, you have run one mile *and* you have not run four
miles. What you did was successfully do what you did. The
next time you will take the next step and build from there.

So, since whatever you did was the best you could do under
the circumstances, and since you succeeded in doing what you
did, then consider it a success. After all, you learned from it,
didn't you? In this way, instead of weighing your mind and
your intelligence down with past errors, you free yourself to
focus on the most suitable way to approach the next step
toward your ultimate goal.

The concept that I have been discussing here—of *doing or not doing* as opposed to *trying and failing*—is one of immense power. Once you understand that when you are doing something it is because you have *chosen* that particular course of action called "doing," you will know that you can choose to "not do" that same thing. Or take the obverse: Once you understand that when you don't do something it is because you have *chosen* that particular course of action called "not doing," you will know that you can choose to "do" that same thing. In other words, you will realize that no person or thing or event is ultimately responsible for the fact that you are doing or not doing something. What this effectively does is put control back where it belongs—with *you.*

The techniques outlined in these pages are designed to help you to develop your awareness of your own capacities and abilities. The very process of carving out a twenty-minute period from each day will enable you to experience on the level of awareness what I am talking about here.

Most of us believe that we are acting freely when we are acting haphazardly. The opposite is true. As Aristotle said, "Freedom is obedience to self-formulated rules." Free choice comes only when we are at cause in a matter, instead of being at the effect of ideas or events or people. And discipline is simply one method we can use in order to develop the qualities necessary for us to realize that we are at cause.

The disciplines that follow are helpful in developing your abilities to adapt and be flexible. It you decide to use them, remember that you are choosing to do so. In other words, approach them positively rather than grudgingly. They represent yet another way in which you can break down habitual approaches to your world, because they introduce a certain arbitrariness into your plans.

The following disciplines will develop your ability to be flexible; each will enable you to develop and strengthen those mental powers that you must have if you are to experience your life as under your own control.

Consider carefully before you decide which of these exercises is not for you. In the case of these particular exercises, you should experience some discomfort or resistance in order to carry them out. After all, the very notion of "discipline" implies something that is somewhat difficult to do. If, on the other hand, you come across something that would be quite comfortable for you, then discard it and choose or create another that would be better.

Self-Disciplines

1. See if you can spend a period of time during the day without talking at all except when you have to answer a direct question. Obviously, the value of the discipline lies in choosing a time when you can be with your usual group, and the point is to achieve this with no one catching on to the fact that anything strange or different is going on. It is a matter of simply not volunteering to talk. You can answer any questions adequately, but you simply stop there, without following up on anything suggested by the exchange and without asking your questioner anything in return. This is much more difficult to achieve than it seems, and one of the things that you will get out of doing this exercise is experiencing how difficult it is to say exactly what we mean when we are answering a question. Usually we blather on for moments at a time trying to clarify what we have originally said.

When you remove yourself from a conversation within a group, there are many other insights that become possible. For example, has the focus of the group shifted in some way? Is someone different doing more talking? Has your relation to the people in the group changed in any way? You may also find that your friends' reactions can be instructive. Whatever realizations you get from this exercise, one result will definitely be that you will feel very different about language. You will have a sense of being in control of it. After a period of self-imposed silence, you will find that when you begin to speak again, you do so with an understanding of the importance of words. You will also know that while you are choosing to speak at the moment, you could just as easily be choosing to be silent.

2. Practice thinking about one subject for a period of time. This is similar to the concentrative meditation exercises, but is really different, and it is very difficult to do. What you do

is choose any concrete object and, after closing your eyes, begin to create it in your imagination. See if you can describe it to yourself. How would each of your senses experience it? Then think about where this particular object comes from. Does it symbolize anything for you? What are its practical uses?

You can try this same exercise focusing your concentration on different aspects of a problem. Here you restrict all of your focus and attention to covering as many aspects of the same problem as you possibly can.

It doesn't matter what kind of object or problem you choose for this exercise. At the beginning, choose something that you feel can hold your interest. But eventually, you should be able to do this concentration discipline by choosing your subjects at random, even by picking them from a newspaper.

Note that this exercise is different from the meditation exercises in which you concentrate exclusively on one thought or phrase or visual input for a period of time. In this exercise, what you are doing is exploring a subject over a period of time.

3. Write a letter that is so interesting that the recipient doesn't realize that you have not once used any of the following words: I, me, my, mine. The person who reads the letter should not even notice that there is anything unusual about it. An interesting result of writing such a letter is that it forces us to turn our focus away from our usual selfish preoccupations. It is astonishing how refreshed we are when we return to our own lives after such an experience.

4. In your conversation or in your letters, see if you can present what is going on for you from a positive point of view. This is not a matter of lying or posing. What is called for here is simply a matter of looking for the positive aspects of what is going on for you at the moment and confining your conversation or your letters to these.

It is usually a pleasant surprise to realize that no matter how bad you may feel, when you look consciously for things that are going well, you discover that there really are some aspects of your life that are going well, but that you have simply been overwhelmed by one particular problem, for example. What this usually does is to put things in a much better perspective.

Another positive result of thinking positively in this way is that it sets off a chain reaction. You may find that your communication with others improves considerably.

5. You have probably heard this advice hundreds of times, and just as probably, you have rarely followed it. This is simply to stop just before you enter a crowded room. You do this expressly to take time to see your relation to the people in the room. Of course, you may think that this is "artificial," and that rushing into a roomful of people represents "spontaneity." On the contrary, by stopping to consider for a moment, you merely ensure that you will not feel overwhelmed by the situation or by the people in the room, that you will not get caught talking to someone who does not interest you only to discover—too late—that the person whom you have been trying to get in touch with all week was just a few steps away. What this does, once again, is to introduce control and choice into the event.

6. The next time you are introduced to someone, see if you can find out as much as possible about him. This discipline involves the idea of turning back any questions that he might ask you and keeping him talking about himself. Again, the person should not realize what you are doing and should not realize that anything unusual is going on. Although this is most valuable when meeting someone new, you can also try it with a friend.

As you concentrate more and more and listen carefully to what this other person is saying, you will find that imperceptively you become genuinely interested in this other person's world, in how things look to him. And, of course, the more your interest and attention become focused, the less self-conscious you will be. Also, when you do finally talk about yourself, you will have a real idea of those things that you could share with this person that would genuinely interest him. This will also save you from the boredom of listening to yourself rattle off the same anecdotes to every new individual that you meet, and from telling the same stories about what-happens-to-be-going-on-at-the-moment to each friend in turn.

Incidentally, when you consciously choose to guide your

conversation in this way, you are not cheating the other person. Just the opposite: You are giving him a chance to deal with his concerns and his interests.

7. In this exercise you do exactly the opposite of what you did in the preceding exercise. Here you intentionally steer the conversation so that you are talking only of what concerns you. Although you may or may not be someone who does this unintentionally, for sure it is very difficult *intentionally* to be this selfish without becoming acutely aware of every reaction that your listener exhibits. By all means try not to bore your listener. And see if you can avoid either boasting or complaining. As you proceed, you will automatically notice if the other person is growing impatient or indifferent or bored. It is a valuable lesson to experience.

One thing that you may become aware of when you do this exercise is the amount of trivial information we usually foist on other people. When we intentionally concentrate on ourselves, rehashing the recurring soap-opera aspects of our lives, the inevitable result is boredom on the part of those who are forced to listen. The positive result of this realization is that it may lead us to seek more interesting and imaginative experiences that we can share with others. This may mean that we have to extend our interests in order to direct our lives so that they become more interesting and exciting and thus more worth sharing with another.

People don't really want to hear the latest installment in your soap opera. And if you find that some of your relationships exist only on this level, you might see if you can consciously guide the conversation to subjects of wider interest or more depth. If you discover that your companion insists on sticking to time-wasting small talk, you may conclude that your friendship and your energy would be placed elsewhere to greater advantage.

To refuse to waste your time and your energy is not cruel. It is simply an obligation that you have to yourself and to your friend. Genuine friendship is stimulating and strengthening. If it is based on trivia, then it is reduced to trivia.

8. Make a plan and stick to it to the exact moment. For this discipline, what you do is plan out a period of time during which you decide to spend, say, exactly ten minutes on some-

thing. And then—no matter how important it seems to continue with it at that moment—when your ten minutes are up, you simply move on to the next scheduled activity. Put some things on the schedule that you would habitually do as well as some things that you have decided need doing. For example, you might schedule exactly how long you'll spend at breakfast and precisely what you will do after that for exactly what period of time and so on. The point of the exercise is to turn to each succeeding activity at the exact moment that you yourself have planned to do so. If you are not quite finished with one item, that is just too bad. Simply move on as scheduled.

It is interesting to experience moving as the result of following our own orders. But, an additional result of this exercise is that you will become aware of just how difficult it is to estimate accurately how long a given task will take. If you have been telling yourself for years that reading the newspaper in the morning was something that you did for just "five minutes," with the intention of filling in later in the day, and you discover that you have been spending half an hour on it, then you have a decision to make. The point is not which way your decision will go, but merely that you should become aware of how you are spending your time. This exercise will awaken in you a new sense of the true value of time.

9. With all of our notions about "free choice," the fact is that most people exhibit astonishing degrees of rigidity in their actions and in their life. One of the ways to develop a sense of flexibility and resiliency is to do this exercise. What is involved is taking some slips of paper and writing down some instructions to yourself. The kinds of assignments that you should choose will vary from individual to individual, but they should be things such as the following:

"Go without food all day."

"Stay up and work through the night."

"Accurately catalogue fifty of the phonograph albums."

I am aware that these kinds of assignments will take more than twenty minutes to carry out, but I have chosen to use them because they are so valuable. If you decide that twenty minutes is really all that you want to devote at this time, then simply create instructions for yourself that fall into that alloted time period. You may discover, however, that the value of this discipline is worth the extra time involved. Besides, it is quite possible to continue with the rest of your routine while not eating or while not saying anything except in answer to questions, so, in that sense, many assignments of this nature do not involve any extra commitment of time on your part.

See if you can come up with at least ten different assignments for yourself which you list on ten different slips of paper. If one particular assignment seems particularly valuable to you, then write it twice by all means. Now, put each paper into its own envelope, seal each envelope, shuffle the pile and put the envelopes away.

On the day that you have chosen to do this discipline, choose one of the envelopes, open it, and do what you have instructed yourself to do. You may have been invited to your parents' fiftieth wedding anniversary on the day that you have picked the envelope that tells you this is the day you are to go without food. Nevertheless, unless you are really ill, you carry out the command and do what you have written on that slip of paper.

In choosing these activities, come up with things that you feel would be of special value to you. Just choose something which cuts into your usual routine in some way so that there is the concept of "discipline" involved.

10. This discipline calls once more for an entire day, but—again—its value is so great that you should seriously consider including it. What is involved is choosing a day from time to time in which you will say "Yes" whenever a reasonable request is made of you. The key here is "reasonable." You can certainly examine and possibly reject the offer of a change of job, for example; but you would have to accept any "reasonable" request even though it might entail some discomfort on your part.

We are so used to habitually saying "No" simply to avoid inconveniencing ourselves or disturbing our routines. Sometimes, by forcing ourselves to say "Yes," we can be surprised by very pleasant consequences and experience something that we would truly have regretted missing.

On the other hand, if you are someone who habitually gets

caught in a round of parties and activities that keep you from doing what is important to you, then you might choose to reverse this exercise and plan to refuse invitations.

Each of us has unique needs, and what is necessary is that you work out disciplines for yourself which will be tailored to your needs specifically. What you need to do is to decide if a particular weakness or performance can be improved by exaggerating what you are doing or by doing the exact opposite.

By the way, although these disciplines can be difficult, they can also be quite amusing as well as helpful, and the insights they provide into the mechanisms of your own behavior can be illuminating. However, it is important to keep in mind that these exercises—as well as all of the exercises in this book—are not goals in and of themselves. That is, they are to be used to train your mind so that you can follow through in your chosen work and become a fully self-actualized person.

Another point that I want to emphasize is that it is of the utmost importance that you begin to take responsibility when you decide *not* to follow through on something. If you have decided that you absolutely will not watch television and then you find that you are watching television (or eating dessert or staying up too late), then notice that what has happened is that you have *decided* to change your mind. It may seem at first that this attitude gives you the liberty to act at random. On the contrary, what it does—to repeat once more—is to place control back in your hands. Once you *get* that the decision is yours and yours alone to make, you are free to choose to do something different from what you are doing—or to continue what you are doing.

And another thing. Recriminations are a waste of everyone's time. On the other hand, consciously noting when you have done what you decided to do and mentally rewarding yourself for a job well done can be a very good way of promoting future proper action. As you continue working on yourself, you will find that your standards have risen. Give yourself the approval you deserve when you meet those standards. Reward yourself. When you don't meet the standards, examine them to make sure they are realistic, note that you *chose* not to meet them this time, or that you came a certain distance towards meeting them, and move on from there.

At this point I would like to return to the formula that was discussed at the beginning of this chapter. In analyzing and breaking down what happens when we act as though our success were virtually assured, it is almost as though we submitted our actions to a slow-motion camera. But when we actually focus our energies in this way, we are released into action from which all extraneous effort has been removed. In other words, the tempo of successful action is smoother than any words about it can demonstrate. Purposeful action always seems clearer, more straightforward and more enjoyable than other kinds of action. You may be working with care and even slower than you would ordinarily, but because there is no confusion, no part of you that is "out to lunch," your feeling about what you are doing will be quite different.

It is this feeling that you are setting out to recapture when you imagine or remember the mood of success. And it is not any objective speed that is being considered, but rather the rhythm that unimpeded movement in a forward direction produces.

Sometimes people reach this understanding through desperation. These are the people who, when faced with catastrophe, can finally mobilize themselves to action. We say of such people that they have nothing to lose. Often individuals will create artificial emergencies for themselves, convinced that that is the only way that they can act. But you do not need desperation; imagination will work even better, and it will leave you facing in the right direction. Once again, the formula is very simple: Act as though your success were virtually assured.

———◀♦▶———

Chapter 23

Habit and Risk
and Responsibility

Experiments have been conducted in which trout and guppies have been placed in a tank with a glass barrier between them. After bashing their heads against the barrier in many unsuccessful attempts to reach their prey, the trout eventually *learn* that they cannot do so. Thereafter, even when the barrier is removed, they will imagine one there and never cross it.

This kind of "learning" is similar to what takes place when we form habits. A habit represents a tendency toward an act that has become, by repeated performance, relatively fixed, consistent, easy, almost automatic.[1] Although we tend to think of our habits in negative terms, as acts that we would like to break ourselves from, the simple fact is that our lives would be intolerable without easy access to habit.

Think about this for a moment. Consider what a triumph it is for a small child to tie his shoelace. If each act that we performed required careful conscious planning on our part, our whole lives might be concerned with mastering one or two such difficulties. So habit can be a good thing. It simplifies our lives and frees us to move on to other things.

In fact, our whole progress in life depends upon the "codes" we have discovered based on our generalizations of our experiences. In other words, we make sense out of what is happening now based upon what we already know and understand from past experience. You can read the message that these words represent only because they are in a language familiar to you. Every phenomenon represents a message, but the message remains a mystery unless you can acquire enough "decoding" information, that is, enough information at a level that you already know and understand, in order to move to the next level.

An example of what I mean may clarify this. When you first learned to write, all your thoughts and efforts had to be aimed at forming the characters correctly. Only when you had sufficiently encapsulated this information, could you begin to think of the thoughts that you wanted to communicate and the style in which you wanted to convey them. You can experience to some degree the distance you have traveled by slowly and laboriously writing your name while concentrating on forming each stroke with painstaking precision. Take a moment to do this—the experience will illustrate my next point: Can you imagine what life would be like if you had never progressed beyond that limit?

Or take another example. What if each time you had to walk from one place to another, you had to first stop and consider which foot to move first and how to lift one and then the other? What if, like a small child, you tottered forward for a few steps only to fall and then have to rise again?

Well, whatever level you are at now, you are doing exactly that. You, yourself, have placed limits on the decoding process and have stopped generalizing from your experience in such a way so as to move to the next higher level.

Habit is neither good nor bad in and of itself: It is merely the way in which we make automatic that which starts out as conscious effort on our part. What can we do both to expand our conceptions of our abilities and to harness the habit-forming ability and make it serve us? That is what this book is about, and there are several ways in which to approach the problem.

One way entails doing whatever we can to become aware of the barriers in our lives that prevent us from functioning at our optimum. We must learn to recognize the "glass walls" that are no longer actual and real (if, in fact, they ever were). Many of the experiential exercises in this book are valuable in working on this. Anything that we can do in order to break down the habitual ways that we perceive can act as a catalyst to the learning experience.

Here are some additional exercises that can be helpful:

1. *Visualizing:* This is slightly different from the exercises in visualization that we have encountered before. What is called for here is the actual turning into a visual experience of something that you have been seeing in verbal or symbolic terms (as in mathematics or music). Take something that is as abstract and difficult as you can, and try to picture it in detail. See if you can fix it at the level of personal experience. What does it mean, specifically, to you?

2. *Reading:* If you are like most people, you read very little beyond what you customarily require just to get by. So much of what is most worthwhile in man's experiences and observations and feelings and aspirations are set down in books. Exposing yourself to this kind of communication can excite you and open you in unforeseen ways. But you needn't start with material that makes you feel uncomfortable. On the contrary, pick your favorite kind of reading material and read a great deal of it. Saturate yourself with knowledge in whatever area interests you. If you do this, you will find that you begin to "encode" what you read, so that you become ready for more sophisticated levels in that field. In addition, your vocabulary will automatically improve.

An interesting experiment that you might want to try is to choose an admirable character that you have been reading about (fictional or nonfictional) and to imagine him in other situations. How would he act? What would he wear? What would he do? As you get more accomplished at this, imagine a character in a situation similar to your own. How would he act? Are his actions and reactions similar to your own? How do they differ? Can you learn anything from seeing how "someone else" acts in a situation similar to yours?

The next stage of this exercise entails putting your fantasy character directly into your circumstances. Give him your desires, your problems. You can either visualize him working out his course of action or you can see yourself asking him for advice. In the chapter on special techniques, there is a more detailed description of this exercise, called "Counselors." For the purpose of this chapter, what I want you to realize is that this kind of fantasy and role-playing works because it gets around the limits that we all place on ourselves. How could we solve such-and-such a problem? It is just too overwhelming. But let us imagine someone whom we respect and admire in just our situation, and quite possibly a solution will reveal itself to us. Sometimes revelations generated by this exercise can be quite startling in their accuracy and helpfulness. What we have been able to achieve, through imagination, is communication with another level of understanding within ourselves.

According to William James, there is another way to make our nervous system our ally instead of our enemy. *"For this we must make automatic and habitual, as early as possible, as many useful actions as we can,* and guard against allowing the formation of disadvantageous habits."[2]

How do we do this? Well, let us return for a moment to our idea of doing things right the first time. According to F. Matthias Alexander, the habitual use of our mechanisms that we bring to our activities is accompanied by certain sensory experiences or feelings which, from their lifelong association with this habitual use, have become familiar to us. Further, from their very familiarity, they have come to "feel right," and so we derive considerable satisfaction from repeating them, even though they may, in fact, not bring the results that we desire. When we try to correct a long-ingrained habit, the correct steps, on the contrary, "feel wrong" to us. In other words, the lure of the familiar will prove too strong for us and will keep us tied down to the habitual use of ourselves that "feels right."[3]

It is therefore imperative that in learning something new we take the time to do it right from the very beginning. Otherwise, we are setting up a very difficult situation for ourselves.

But what about those undesirable habits we have already acquired? Well, James says that we should launch ourselves with a strong and decided initiative to change a habit and that we should "never suffer an exception to occur till the new habit is securely rooted in [our lives]."[4] This, of course, brings us to the question of *will.*

The majority of our actions are involuntary movements that occur automatically and reflexively. What we are looking at now are those acts which are voluntary on our part. The concept of volition leads us to what James calls the "fiat," the element of consent or resolve that is necessary if the act is to ensue. This element of consent is what constitutes the essence of what we mean by the voluntariness of the act.

In all unhesitating voluntary acts, the idea of the consequences or end of the act will be all that is necessary to begin the sequence of events that will result in the act's accomplishment. And the more we concern ourselves with the end rather than any particular means to that end, the more likely we are to achieve it with accuracy and certainty. (It is easier to catch a thrown ball if we think only of catching the ball and not at all about what to do with our hands and feet.)

Sometimes an idea is sufficient to spur us on to action, but "sometimes an additional conscious element, in the shape of a fiat, mandate, or express consent, has to intervene and precede the movement."[5] But what is it that permits certain ideas to manifest themselves so easily in the world of reality, while other acts require this extra express consent? According to James, it "seems to be *the absence of any conflicting notion in the mind.*"[6] Where there are no conflicts, nothing intervenes between the thought and the action. Every moment of our lives is filled with thoughts and ideas and possibilities. Where no conflicting image presents itself, movement is the natural immediate effect of the process.

But what happens when there are conflicting forces? It is then that we have our decisions. James discusses different kinds of decisions, beginning with those that are the result of our reasoning out of options and including those that are reached through "awakenings of conscience" or conversions. Most of these, like most human decisions, are decisions without effort. The feeling of effort that is present in comparatively few of them is what we generally refer to when we speak of willpower. This willpower may be necessary either to spur on action or to inhibit action. And it is this effort that complicates volition. "It does so whenever a rarer and more ideal impulse is called upon to neutralize others of a more instinctive and habitual kind; it does so whenever strongly explosive tendencies are checked, or strongly obstructive conditions overcome."[7] And what determines the amount of effort is simply the greatness of the resistance itself.

On a practical level, then, what should we do when we become the victim of opposing thoughts? If it is true that "what holds attention determines action,"[8] then anything that we can do to compel attention to an idea will aid in freeing ourselves for action. This is not to say that our acts will always be successful, but only that once we make an idea prevail in the mind, we have gotten out of our own way.

And how do we make an idea prevail? *"The essential achievement of the will . . . is to attend to a difficult object and hold it fast before the mind. The so-doing is the fiat. . . . Effort of attention is the essential phenomenon of will."*[9] All this has nothing to do with physical or muscular effort. The difficulty is mental, and what is involved is the notion of facing an idea as real.

For James, the strong willed man is the one who affirms an idea, consents to its presence, and holds it fast, despite the hundreds of opposing mental images which rise to expel it from the mind.

> Sustained in this way by a resolute effort of attention, the difficult object erelong begins to call up its own congeners and associates and ends by changing the disposition of the man's consciousness altogether. And with his consciousness his action changes, for the new object, once stably in possession of the field of his thoughts, infallibly produces its own motor effect. The difficulty lies in the gaining possession of that field. . . .
>
> *Consent to the idea's undivided presence, this is effort's sole achievement . . .* and for this there is but one way. The idea to be consented to must be kept from flickering and going out. It must be held steadily before the mind until it *fills* the mind. Such filling of the mind by an idea *is* consent to the idea. . . . [and] the deepest question that is ever asked admits of no reply but the dumb turning of the heart strings as we say, *"Yes, I will even have it so!"*[10]

Anything that we can do to train our abilities in the direction of better concentration will greatly facilitate the control we are able to manifest in this area. My suggestion would be to use the meditation techniques to this end, as well as the exercises in creative imagination. Training ourselves to focus in on one thought, practicing the visualization of desired ends —both of these processes will prepare us so that when we have need to call on the power of our will, it will be there to serve us.

We now come to a concept that is fundamental to the understanding of this book. It has been mentioned before—for example, in the discussion of self-actualizing individuals—but I believe that it requires further exploration. What I am leading up to is the concept of responsibility.

Of what value is your consent or fiat if you have no control over what happens, if what happens to you is the result of someone else's actions? It is not my intention to get into a philosophical discussion on the question of free will as opposed to determinism. It seems obvious that a definitive answer to whether our acts are fully determined or not is impossible. It then comes down to a matter of choice: It is true that every act and every thought that you have may be fully predetermined, but it is also possible that they may not be, and I suggest that your life will be immeasurably enriched to the degree that you are willing to accept responsibility for it.

Many of the techniques in this book are aimed at awakening in you a consciousness and awareness of your own powers and capabilities. If you work on them consistently, you will come to feel less and less that you are at the effect of events and people and ideas.

Responsibility begins with the willingness to acknowledge that you are the source and the cause in a matter. Werner Erhard says that it starts with the willingness to deal with a situation from and with the point of view—whether at the moment realized or not—that you are the source of what you are, what you do and what you have. Responsibility has certain characteristics that are reminiscent of the witness that we encountered in the meditation exercise in that, when you view things from the point of view of responsibility, you do not praise or blame. The viewpoint of responsibility leaves out judgments and evaluations concerning good and bad, or right and wrong or better and worse. Responsibility is a simple acknowledgement that you are cause in your own experience. Erhard extends this concept to include even what is done to you, and ultimately what another does to another.

Of course, this is all part of another dichotomy, but the closer you come to accepting your responsibility in the creation of your own experience, the more willing you are to take that point of view, the more likely you will come to transcending the seemingly irreconcilable aspects.

And, talking about your experience of what happens, you can certainly choose to make that a positive thing. All it takes is the recognition that whatever happens, happens separately from what you add to it by deciding it was either good or bad. Reality is neither good nor bad; it just is. And your willingness to have it be that way and to be responsible for your experience of it can uncover layer upon layer of new possibilities.

---◀◆▶---

Chapter 24

How To Use
This Book

If you have followed the suggestion at the beginning of this
book, then you have arrived at this chapter by reading in a
series of concentrated intervals up to this point. You may have
come across some ideas that you could immediately assimilate
—such as those suggested for remembering new people—but
basically you have read through the book in a focused fashion.
If you have done this, then you already have a feeling about
what even short periods of total concentration can mean in
terms of your abilities and capacities. Hopefully, you have
become interested enough to want to follow through so that
you can tap into a more powerful intelligence.

In one sense, this will be easy; after all, you need never take
more than twenty minutes a day. However, as you have probably already realized, the consistent commitment of even so
brief a period of time can be difficult. The exercises in this
book will help you in this, although the very simplicity of some
of them may prove a stumbling block. They are not difficult
to understand or to do once or twice; the hard part comes in
allowing yourself to experience them over and over again at
deeper and deeper levels of awareness. It can be somewhat
frightening to open ourselves up to new experiences. But if
you know this at the beginning, you should be able to push
through your considerations to the exciting discoveries that
lie at the other end.

The one thing that I can tell you for sure is that you don't have much time. People continually live their lives as though they were practicing for the next time around, when the simple fact is that when today is over it will be gone forever and there will be no way to make it up. Tomorrow doesn't exist, so no matter what you intend to do tomorrow, if you have wasted all your todays, you will have lost your life. This is quite different from planning for tomorrow: What planning actually is is doing today and living today. If you fully live your todays, your tomorrows will take care of themselves and you will never have to regret your yesterdays.

So, now you have read most of this book. Probably you feel a little overwhelmed by all the input; probably, too, you feel that you pretty well understand what I have been getting at. If you now put the book aside, I can only tell you that you will have cheated yourself of a great deal, because this book is only indirectly concerned with understanding. Mostly it is about experiencing—about expanding awareness and increasing perception. And you can't do that by reading about it: You must live it.

Some of you may be excited by what you've read and may have decided in your minds to attack several fronts at once and become "perfect." If that is what you're thinking, I can assure you that you have probably guaranteed the only other way that you can fail with these exercises. To repeat, the techniques that I have described here are not meant to be read, understood, and tried once or twice. And you don't get a medal for racing through every one of them in order to check each off on some imaginary list. On the contrary, each is meant to be savored.

What this means in practice is that once again you are called upon to choose. You may take everything in the order that I have presented it, or you may decide to begin somewhere in the middle. That is not what matters. What is crucial, however, is that you allow yourself to go deeply into whatever area you have chosen. This may mean that you do one exercise for twenty minutes, that you feel that you can get more out of that one exercise, and that you therefore choose to work on that one exercise for an entire week or more. Not every exercise will interest you to the same degree, but you should be open to that possibility with all of them. In other words, there is no rush to complete all the exercises. If I could choose between your casually experiencing most of the techniques or deeply experiencing a few of them, there is no question in my mind which I would choose. By concentrating on one thing at a time, you will be learning at the intuitive as well as the rational level, and that is what genuine learning is about.

What I would suggest as a starting point would be to take a few moments to thumb through this book, noting down on a pad those exercises or sections that seem to have particular meaning for you. Even this is not something that you will have to figure out logically. Go with your feelings about which areas seem to hold the most for you. Go through the entire book in this way. When you finish, you will probably have too many exercises listed to work on at once. Fine. What this gives you a chance to do is to set priorities for yourself. Remember that you are the one who is setting these priorities and that you are free to change your mind as your needs change.

Just for now, rank the items on your list in the importance they hold for you at this moment, and decide that you will work on the first one or the first two or three. More than this will prove unworkable. What you will be doing then, in practice, is using your twenty-minute periods to work on one or another of the areas that you have decided are most important to you at this time.

If possible, see if you can balance your choices so that, for example, you might spend part of your twenty minutes on a visualization exercise, part on a breathing exercise and part on a body exercise. At the beginning, especially, you may want to sample in this way. Also, you may not be able to sustain concentration on any one exercise for the whole twenty minutes. On the other hand, remain open to the possibility that you may get so deeply into an exercise that the twenty minutes will be over before you realize it. Fine. These techniques are meant to be explored by you and for you. Do not set up any artificial standards that you must meet in doing them. All that is necessary is your willingness to do whatever you do in as complete a manner as you possibly can. The changes that occur will be subtle ones. Be open to them. Be willing to experience . . . and experience again.

If you find that you experience something special with a particular technique, note down your realizations. Plan to return to that technique again. And know that the doing of the exercises described in these pages will have a cumulative effect: Each time that you experience them, you will do so on a progressively deeper level of awareness.

Another thing: By sticking to fairly regular twenty-minute intervals, you will have set a goal for yourself that is challenging but attainable. You may want to believe *now* that you will devote three hours a day to these techniques, but how long do you think such an unrealistic schedule would last in the face of everyday reality? On the other hand, twenty minutes is a possible amount of time to carve out for yourself. It is a long enough amount of time to represent a commitment on your part, yet even on especially busy days you can fulfill that commitment since you can decide to do the exercises that are designed to fit into the smallest chunks of time on those days.

Some people never reach beyond what is safe for them and thus insure that they will be bored. Some people continually set unrealistic goals for themselves and thus guarantee that they will fail. By setting a challenging, yet reasonable amount of time—and I believe that twenty minutes is that amount— and by carrying through daily on your commitment, you virtually assure that you will succeed.

Remember that what we are dealing with here is education that arrives at a different perception of self, and although insights may come suddenly, they cannot be programmed. This is another kind of education; that is, experiential education. And its premise is that what is necessary to change a person is to change his awareness of himself.[1]

The biggest trap that you could fall into as you work with this book would be to figure it out and to understand it. On the contrary, by *doing* and *experiencing* the kinds of exercises presented here, you can "become aware of internal, subjective, subverbal experiences, so that these experiences can be brought into the world of abstraction, of conversation, of communication, of naming, etc., with the consequence that it immediately becomes possible for a certain amount of control to be exerted over these hitherto unconscious and uncontrollable processes."[2] In short, that you will have taken twenty minutes a day to a more powerful intelligence.

Chapter 25

In Conclusion . . . A Beginning

In this book, I have wanted to share techniques with you that could be useful in expanding your awareness of your potentialities. It has never been my intention to show you ways to change yourself. When you try to change something about yourself, you are trying to manipulate a part of you, and naturally part of you will resist the change. Usually, the more you resist, the more fixed you will become in the very thing that you wish to change.

This book, on the contrary, is predicated on the notion that it is more helpful that you become deeply aware of yourself *just as you are now*. As you begin to experience yourself as you are, change takes place by itself, without effort on your part. The exercises I have outlined are those which will help get you out of your own way, will enable you to focus and concentrate, and will help you to expand your parameters of understanding and experience. I have wanted to show you ways to tune in to your own special reality, to find out those things which are most precious to you, and I have wanted to demonstrate ways in which you can free yourself of negative and unrealistic limits which you may have placed on your possibilities.

What follows is a brief summary of some of the more important points that I hope you will have experienced through my words and the doing of the exercises discussed:

1. Until you have decided on a goal (or the results you want), you cannot plan to attain it. Further, you are not free to change your mind about your goal until you have first made a decision.

2. Successful people do not get stuck in the past; nor do they live in a fantasied future: They create in the present moment.

3. A strongly visualized intention carries its own force—an energy that clarifies and illuminates.

4. Self-actualizers manage somehow simultaneously to love the world as it is and to work to improve it. In the same way, they somehow accept themselves while they work to develop themselves.

5. Self-actualizers experience the "suchness" of things. " 'Suchness' is a synonym for the Japanese word *sonomama*. . . . Literally it means the 'is-it-isness' of things. . . . [It] refers to the peculiar and characteristic defining whole-quality, or Gestalt, of an object which makes it exactly what it is," and not anything else. It is that which "differentiates it from everything else in the whole world."[1]

6. You can have your considerations and still do what you want. By experiencing yourself on deeper levels of awareness, you can transcend the dichotomy between that which is vulnerable in you and that which is strong, as well as that which is self and that which is other.

7. We add immeasurably to our lives when we place the intuitive and experiential beside the rational and logical and give both sides of our nature their due. The synthesis that results permits an experience of self that far surpasses what either alone can provide.

8. Keeping in mind the concept of *synergy,* it is possible to be selfish and altruistic at the same time.

9. Within every person, to some degree, there exist needs beyond those at the basic-need level. "In certain definable and empirical ways, it is [as] necessary for man to live in beauty rather than ugliness, as it is necessary for him to have food for an aching belly or rest for a weary body."[2] In fact, these metaneeds represent the very meaning of life although they are below the level of awareness of most people.

10. When you take responsibility for your own experience,

you do not judge or evaluate or praise or fix blame. You simply acknowledge that you are the source of what you are, what you do and what you have.

11. One of the ways we can free ourselves to act is simply to imagine what we would do if it really were impossible for us to fail and then to act as though this were true.

12. Completion leads to satisfaction. One accomplishment in the real world is worth a mountain of dreams.

13. Sometimes the deepest insights result from deceptively simple procedures. The most difficult aspect about some of the exercises in this book is their very simplicity. At the same time, if you continue to experience them with consistency, their effect is cumulative.

14. Do not settle for understanding this book: Experience it.

The texture of this book is complex. There are contradictions and paradoxes represented in these pages. That is because the truth is pluralistic, and you must grasp each concept within the context in which it is presented. If you can permit yourself to accept the variety possible in mental life, you are on your way to experiencing that variety and thereby expanding your consciousness.

Has this book succeeded? You can easily apply a pragmatic test for yourself. Has reading this book and doing these exercises in some way changed the way in which you experience yourself, your capabilities, your possibilities? Have your horizons enlarged? Has your comprehension improved? Are you in some way aware of yourself on a deeper level of understanding and responsibility? If so, then you are moving closer to realizing a more powerful intelligence.

Remember that when your aim is one of self-actualization, there are certain characteristics that you will exhibit:

First, you will want to experience fully in the present moment, realizing that self-fulfillment is an ongoing process in which life is embraced as a series of choices in which one opts, always, for the growth choice.

Second, you will want to engage in any behavior that will allow you to tune into whatever your personal inner voices reveal is true for you.

Third, you will want to set up conditions so that you are

more likely to experience insights and cognitions, and you will realize that these must be followed and backed up by periods of hard work.

And fourth, you will want to accept and embrace the notion of being responsible for your experience of your life.

Intelligence represents a combination of aptitudes, acquired knowledge and potentialities. It is not a static thing that stops developing because someone fastens an Intelligent Quotient number on it. Intelligence, in fact, is much like a muscle whose strength grows with use. In short, the outer parameters of intelligence are determined only by your willingness to test them. This, as we have discussed before, means commitment and hard work. But the rewards are limitless and exciting. There is no ending to this process except one that is self-imposed. Let this book represent a place to begin.

Notes

Chapter 1

1. Horace B. English and Ava Champney English, eds., *A Comprehensive Dictionary of Psychological and Psychoanalytical Terms* (New York: Longmans, Green & Co., 1958), pp. 267–269.

2. Abraham Maslow, *The Farther Reaches of Human Nature* (New York: The Viking Press, 1971), pp. 41–53.

3. See Abraham Maslow, *Religions, Values, and Peak-Experiences* (New York: Penguin Books, 1970).

4. Alexander Lowen, *Pleasure: A Creative Approach to Life* (New York: Penguin Books, 1970), p. 148.

5. David McClelland at Harvard-M.I.T., among others.

6. David McClelland, "That Urge to Achieve," in *Organizational Psychology, a Book of Readings,* 2nd ed. David A. Kolb, Irwin M. Rubin, James M. McIntyre, eds. (Englewood Cliffs, N. J.: Prentice-Hall, 1971), p. 148.

7. Ibid., p. 152.

8. Ibid., p. 153.

Chapter 3

1. William James, "The Energies of Men," in *Memories and Studies* (London: Longmans Green & Co., 1911), as reprinted in *Vogue* (January, 1969), p. 128.

2. Ibid., p. 127.

Chapter 4

1. See Robert R. Blake and Jane S. Mouton, *The Management Grid* (Houston, Texas: Gulf Publishing Co., 1964).

2. Joseph A. Litterer, *The Analysis of Organizations* (New York: John Wiley & Sons, 1973), p. 106.

3. Sheldon S. Zalkind and Timothy W. Costello, "Perception: Implications for Administration," *Administrative Quarterly,* VII (September, 1962), pp. 218–35.

4. David A. Kolb, Irwin M. Rubin, and James J. McIntyre, *Organizational Psychology: An Experiential Approach,* 2nd ed. (Englewood Cliffs, N. J.: Prentice-Hall, 1974), pp. 213–228.

Chapter 5

1. For further study in this area, see Herbert Benson, *The Relaxation Response* (New York: William Morrow, 1975).

2. Robert E. Ornstein, *The Psychology of Consciousness* (New York: The Viking Press, 1972), p. 107.

3. Abraham Maslow, *Religions, Values, and Peak-Experiences* (New York: The Viking Press, 1972), p. 59.

4. Ornstein, *The Psychology of Consciousness,* p. 132.

5. Arthur Deikman, "Experimental Meditation," *Journal of Nervous and Mental Disorders, 136* (1963), pp. 329–343.

6. B. Anand, G. Chhina, and B. Singh, "Studies on Shri Ramananda Yogi During His Stay in an Airtight Box," *Indian Journal of Medical Research, 49* (1961), pp. 82–89. Ornstein, *The Psychology of Consciousness,* pp. 130, 131, 196–199. See also Gerald Jonas, *Visceral Learning* (New York: The Viking Press, 1973).

7. Ornstein, *The Psychology of Consciousness,* p. 130.

8. See K. M. Bykov and W. H. Gantt, *The Cerebral Cortex and the Internal Organs* (New York: Chemical Publishing Co., 1975).

9. See T. Barber et al., eds., *Biofeedback and Self-Control* (Chicago: Aldine-Atherton, 1971).

10. David P. Nowlis and J. Kamiya, "The Control of Electroencephalographic Alpha Rhythms through Auditory Feedback and the Associated Mental Activity," *Psychophysiology* 6, no. 4 (1970), pp. 476–484. See also Jonas, *Visceral Learning.*

11. Roy M. Pritchard, "Stabilized Images on the Retina," *Scientific American* (June, 1961), pp. 72–78. D. Lehmann, G. W. Beeler, and D. H. Fender, "EEG Responses During the Observation of Stabilized and Normal Retinal Images," *Electroencephalography and Clinical Neurophysiology, 22* (1967), pp. 136–142. W. Cohen, "Spatial and Textural Characteristics of the Ganzfeld," *American Journal of Psychology, 70* (1957), pp. 403–410. T. C. Cadwallander, "Cessation of Visual Experience under Prolonged Uniform Visual Stimulation," *American Psychologist, 13* (1958), 410 (abstract).

12. Ornstein, *The Psychology of Consciousness,* p. 214.
13. Ibid., p. 178.

Chapter 6

1. Horace B. English and Ava Champney English, eds., *A Comprehensive Dictionary of Psychological and Psychoanalytical Terms* (New York: Longmans, Green & Co., 1958), p. 315.
2. Richard C. Atkinson and Richard M. Shiffrin, "The Control of Short-Term Memory," *Scientific American* (August, 1971), pp. 82–90.
3. Ibid., p. 86.
4. William James, *Psychology: The Briefer Course* (New York: Harper Torchbooks, 1961), p. 161.
5. See S. Woodworth, *Psychology,* 3rd ed. (New York: Henry Holt & Co., 1934).
6. A very helpful commonsense approach to memory and memory systems is provided by James D. Weinland, *How to Improve Your Memory* (New York: Barnes and Noble, 1957).
7. English and English, eds., *Psychological Terms,* p. 225.
8. Harry Lorayne and Jerry Lucas, *The Memory Book* (New York: Ballantine Books, 1974), p. 86.

Chapter 7

1. Horace B. English and Ava Champney English, eds., *A Comprehensive Dictionary of Psychological and Psychoanalytical Terms* (New York: Longmans, Green & Co., 1958), pp. 99–100.
2. See especially Francis P. Robinson, *Effective Study* (New York: Harper & Bros. Publishers, 1946). Despite early date of publication, this is still one of the best "study books" available.

Chapter 8

1. Experiments conducted by Dr. Johnson O'Connor at the Human Engineering Laboratory of Boston and the Stevens Institute of Technology, Hoboken, N. J.

Chapter 10

1. Horace B. English and Ava Champney English, eds., *A Comprehensive Dictionary of Psychological and Psychoanalytical Terms* (New York: Longmans, Green & Co., 1958), p. 253.

Chapter 13

1. Horace B. English and Ava Champney English, eds., *A Comprehensive Dictionary of Psychological and Psychoanalytical Terms* (New York: Longmans, Green & Co., 1958), p. 573.

Chapter 14

1. Frederick S. Perls, *Gestalt Therapy Verbatim* (New York: Bantam Books, 1972), p. 5.
2. Alexander Lowen, *The Betrayal of the Body* (New York: Collier Books, 1975), pp. 209–210.
3. Ibid., p. 231.

Chapter 15

1. Puente-Dominguez and R. Dominguez in the 1950s (as reported in *Summary* VIII, 1956).
2. See Ben Feingold, *Why Your Child Is Hyperactive* (New York: Random House, 1957).
3. George Watson, *Nutrition and Your Mind* (New York: Harper and Row, 1972), p. 88.
4. Ibid., pp. 76–82.
5. Ibid., pp. 94 and 98.
6. Ibid., p. 145.
7. Robert E. Ornstein, *The Psychology of Consciousness* (New York: The Viking Press, 1972), p. 124.
8. W. H. Bates, *Better Eyesight Without Glasses* (New York: Pyramid Books, 1965), p. 90.

Chapter *16*

1. Douglas M. McGregor, 5th Anniversary Convocation, School of Industrial Management, Massachusetts Institute of Technology, Cambridge, Mass.
2. Abraham Maslow, *The Farther Reaches of Human Nature* (New York: The Viking Press, 1971), p. 300.
3. Ibid., p. 310.
4. Ibid., p. 315.
5. Abraham Maslow, *Eupsychian Management* (Homewood, Ill.: Richard D. Irwin and the Dorsey Press, 1965), p. xi.
6. Ibid., p. xi.
7. Ibid., p. xi.
8. Ibid., p. 250.
9. Ibid., p. 250.
10. Ibid., p. 254.
11. Ibid., p. 254.
12. Ruth Benedict, as quoted in Maslow, *Human Nature*, p. 202.
13. Maslow, *Eupsychian*, p. 256.

Chapter *17*

1. See, for example, Bernard Haldane, *Career Satisfaction and Success* (New York: AMACOM, 1974).
2. Ibid., p. 37.
3. Ibid., p. 37.

Chapter *18*

1. Alan Lakein, *How To Get Control of Your Time and Your Life* (New York: Peter H. Wyden, 1973), p. 22.
2. Ibid., p. 117.
3. Ibid., p. 45.
4. Ibid., p. 54.

Chapter *19*

1. Arthur Whimbey, "You Can Learn to Raise Your IQ Score," *Psychology Today* (January, 1976), p. 27.
2. Ibid., p. 85.

Chapter 20

1. See Edward de Bono, *Lateral Thinking* (New York: Harper & Row, 1973).
2. Ibid., p. 68.
3. Ibid., p. 70.
4. Ibid., p. 86.

Chapter 21

1. And see Abraham Maslow, *The Farther Reaches of Human Nature* (New York: The Viking Press, 1971).
2. Ibid., p. 91.
3. Ibid., p. 65.

Chapter 22

1. Abraham Maslow, *The Farther Reaches of Human Nature* (New York: The Viking Press, 1971), pp. 67–68.

Chapter 23

1. Horace B. English and Ava Champney English, eds., *A Comprehensive Dictionary of Psychological and Psychoanalytical Terms* (New York: Longmans, Green & Co., 1958), p. 235.
2. William James, *Psychology, the Briefer Course* (New York: Harper Torchbooks, 1961), p. 11.
3. F. Matthias Alexander, *The Use of the Self* (London: Re-Educational Publications Limited, 1955), p. 34.
4. James, *Psychology, the Brifer Course,* p. 12.
5. Ibid., p. 290.
6. Ibid., p. 291.
7. Ibid., p. 309.
8. Ibid., p. 315.
9. Ibid., p. 317.
10. Ibid., pp. 319–320; p. 326.

Chapter 24

1. Abraham Maslow, *Religions, Values, and Peak-Experiences* (New York: The Viking Press, 1964), p. 89.
2. Ibid., p. 90.

Chapter 25

1. Abraham Maslow, *The Farther Reaches of Human Nature* (New York: The Viking Press, 1971), p. 251.
2. Ibid., p. 44.

Bibliography

Alexander, F. Matthias. *The Use of the Self.* London: Re-Educational Publications Ltd., 1957.

Anderson, U. S., *The Magic in Your Mind.* Hollywood, Calif.: Wilshire Book Co., 1966.

Atkinson, Richard C., and Shiffrin, Richard M. "The Control of Short-Term Memory." *Scientific American* (August, 1971), pp. 82–90.

Bates, W. H. *Better Eyesight Without Glasses.* New York: Pyramid Books, 1965.

Benson, Herbert. *The Relaxation Response.* New York: William Morrow, 1975.

Blake, Robert R., and Mouton, Jane S. *The Management Grid.* Houston, Texas: Gulf Publishing Co., 1964.

Bolles, Richard Nelson. *What Color Is Your Parachute?* Berkeley, Calif.: Ten Speed Press, 1973.

Bykov, K. M., and Gantt, W. H. *The Cerebral Cortex and the Internal Organs.* New York: Chemical Publishing Co., 1975.

Clark, Linda. *Get Well Naturally.* New York: Arc Books, 1972.

Cohen, W. "Spatial and Textural Characteristics of the Ganzfeld." *American Journal of Psychology* 70 (1957), pp. 403–10.

De Bono, Edward. *Lateral Thinking.* New York: Harper and Row, 1973.

Deikman, Arthur. "Experimental Meditation." *Journal of Nervous and Mental Disorders* 136 (1963), pp. 329–43.

English, Horace B., and English, Ava C., eds. *Dictionary of Psychological and Psychoanalytical Terms.* New York: Longmans, Green and Co., 1958.

Feingold, Ben. *Why Your Child Is Hyperactive.* New York: Random House, 1975.

Haldane, Bernard. *Career Satisfaction and Success.* New York: AMACOM, 1974.

Hewitt, James. *Yoga and You.* New York: Pyramid Books, 1968.

James, Muriel, and Jongeward, Dorothy. *Born to Win.* Reading, Mass.: Addison-Wesley Publishing, 1973.

James, William. "The Energies of Men" in *Memories and Studies*. London: Longmans Green & Co., 1911. Reprinted in *Vogue* (January, 1969), pp. 126–70.

————. *Psychology: The Briefer Course*. New York: Harper Torchbooks, 1961.

Jonas, Gerald. *Visceral Learning*. New York: The Viking Press, 1973.

Keleman, Stanley. *Living Your Dying*. New York: Random House, 1974.

Kelly, Howard H. "Two Functions of Reference Groups" in *Readings in Social Psychology*. New York: Holt, Rinehart & Co., 1952.

Kolb, David A.; Rubin, Irwin M.; and McIntyre, James J., eds. *Organizational Psychology: A Book of Readings*. 2nd ed. Englewood Cliffs, N. J.: Prentice-Hall, 1974.

————. *Organizational Psychology: An Experiential Approach*. 2nd ed. Englewood Cliffs, N. J.: Prentice-Hall, 1973.

Lakein, Alan. *How to Get Control of Your Time and Your Life*. New York: Peter H. Wyden, Inc., 1973.

Litterer, Joseph A. *The Analysis of Organizations*. 2nd ed. New York: John Wiley & Sons, 1973.

Lorayne, Harry, and Lucas, Jerry. *The Memory Book*. New York: Ballantine Books, 1974.

Lowen, Alexander. *The Betrayal of the Body*. New York: Collier Books, 1975.

————. *Pleasure: A Creative Approach to Life*. New York: Penguin Books, 1975.

Maltz, Maxwell. *Psycho-Cybernetics*. New York: Pocket Books, 1966.

Marrow, Alfred. *Behind the Executive Mask*. New York: American Management Association, 1964.

Maslow, Abraham. *Eupsychian Management*. Homewood, Ill.: Richard D. Irwin and the Dorsey Press, 1965.

————. *The Farther Reaches of Human Nature*. New York: The Viking Press, 1971.

————. *Religions, Values, and Peak-Experiences*. New York: The Viking Press, 1972.

Massarik, Fred, and Wechsler, Irving. "Empathy Revisited: The Process of Understanding People" in *California Management Review* I, no. 2, pp. 36–46.

Montgomery, Ruth. *Born to Heal*. New York: Popular Library, 1973.

Newburger, Howard and Lee, Marjorie. *Winners and Losers*. New York: David McKay & Co., 1974.

Nowlis, David, and Kamiya, J. "The Control of Electroencephalographic Alpha Rhythms through Auditory Feedback and the Associated Mental Activity." *Psychophysiology* 6, no. 4 (1970), pp. 476–84.

Ornstein, Robert E. *The Psychology of Consciousness.* New York: The Viking Press, 1972.

Ousby, William. *Self-Hypnosis and Scientific Self-Suggestion.* New York: Arc Books, 1969.

Perls, Frederick S. *Gestalt Therapy Verbatim.* New York: Bantam Books, 1972.

———. *In and Out the Garbage Pail.* New York: Bantam Books, 1972.

Pritchard, Roy. "Stabilized Images on the Retina." *Scientific American* (June, 1961), pp. 72–78.

Robinson, Francis P. *Effective Study.* New York: Harper & Bros. Publishers, 1946.

Sivananda, Swami Sri. *Science of Pranayama.* Durban, South Africa: Divine Life Society, 1964.

Smith, Adam. *Powers of Mind.* New York: Random House, 1975.

Vishnudevananda, Swami. *The Complete Illustrated Book of Yoga.* New York: Bell Publishing Company, Inc., 1959.

Watson, George. *Nutrition and Your Mind.* New York: Harper and Row, 1972.

Weinland, James D. *How to Improve Your Memory.* New York: Barnes and Noble, 1957.

Whimbey, Arthur. "You Can Learn to Raise Your IQ Score." *Psychology Today* (January, 1976), pp. 27–85.

Wood, Ernest. *Concentration: An Approach to Meditation.* Wheaton, Ill: The Theosophical Publishing House, 1970.